D1008888

the
GOLDEN RULES
FOR MANAGERS

119 INCREDIBLE LESSONS FOR
LEADERSHIP SUCCESS

FRANK McNAIR

SOURCEBOOKS, INC.®
NAPERVILLE, ILLINOIS

"Leave it to Frank to make you smack yourself on the forehead again and again with 'That's brilliant!' Full of *practical*, good stuff you'll use every day!"
—Jerry Hancock, Managing Partner
Alexander Hancock Associates

"Frank McNair, who I have been privileged to engage for nearly 20 years, provides tools that are actually usable by all level of managers. He remains the one consistent part of our entire training approach."
—Jeff Mick, President
Amarr Garage Doors

"Frank gets it! Many other management and leadership consultants do not. Several years ago I went to a bookstore and purchased 11 books on management and leadership. I read them all. Frank's resonated with me more because it had the most common sense, was the most executable and the most achievable. Frank has worked with our team on an on-going basis through one- and two-day seminars since then."
—Larry Connor, President and CEO
The Connor Group

"If Frank McNair writes it...Read It! His writing is filled with sales and management pearls that can help anyone at any level within your organization."
—Arthur A. Geary, President
Halpern Eye Associates

"The field managers in our company look to this book for real world approaches to leading their team. It's a book that can be referred to again and again."
—Mike McQuiston, Partner
The Connor Group

"Frank has a gift for distilling profound management wisdom into pithy, memorable, and often humorous nuggets. The managers that he teaches and the readers of his books come away with a treasure trove of practical advice on how to be more successful. Frank's passion for his subject and for his clients' success comes through in every line."
—Emmie H. Alexander, Partner
AlexanderHancock Associates

"As a Senior Vice President I have found Frank McNair's management insights and perspectives of running an organization extremely insightful."
—Marty Krcelic, Senior Vice President
TBC Corporation

"Frank McNair has captured the true essence of leadership in this inspiring book. In today's competitive business environment it is essential to master leadership skills. McNair provides an invaluable resource for doing just that!"
—Charles R. Pruett, CLU, Managing Partner
The Pruett Financial Group, Northwestern Mutual Financial Network

"Frank McNair can help any manager who works in a highly diverse work environment get better productivity from his or her associates. This book will allow you as a manager to get the results and productivity needed to make an impact in today's ever changing business world."
—Tim Washinski, Food & Beverage Manager
Kessler Collection Hotels/ Resorts

Published by Sourcebooks, Inc.
P.O. Box 4410, Naperville, Illinois 60567-4410
(630) 961-3900
Fax: (630) 961-2168
www.sourcebooks.com

Originally published in 2000 by AMACOM.

Library of Congress Cataloging-in-Publication Data

McNair, Frank.
  The golden rules for managers : 119 incredible lessons for leadership success /
Frank McNair.
     p. cm.
  Originally published: New York : AMACON, 2000.
  1. Leadership. 2. Management. 3. Success in business. I. Title.
  HD57.7.M3992 2009
  658.4'092—dc22
                                2009003444

Printed and bound in the United States of America
BG 10 9 8 7 6 5 4 3 2 1

For Laura, who has lived with me as I have learned these maxims and put up with me as I have tried to shape them into a book.

You are a superb business partner, a gifted trainer, and a splendid colleague. Beyond that, you are a wonderful spiritual companion and the love of my life. And you are my best friend. I am richly blessed. Thanks.

CONTENTS

ACKNOWLEDGMENTS

I t is impossible for any writer to acknowledge fully his debt to those who have coached, cajoled, mentored, and taught him. And it is particularly impossible in the case of a book like this—where much of the learning has been received from the oral tradition and the tribal lore of management.

I am indebted to all those who—over the years—have allowed me to work with and for them as an employee. Except in rare instances of direct quotation, I have changed your stories to respect your privacy. But you know who you are.

More even than my employers, I thank the clients who have allowed me to bring these life lessons and management lessons to the workplaces they oversee. In the crucible of daily management, these maxims have been tempered by the fire of reality. Thank you for sharing your stories, your insight, and your maxims.

Finally, I thank the colleagues with whom I have worked as a trainer and consultant; you will find yourselves in here often. Thank you for all you taught me and for sharing with me in this search for the tribal lore of the species *managementus uprightus*.

No project of this magnitude ever comes to fruition without the love and attention of a caring agent and an editor with an eye on deadlines. I thank Andrea Pedolsky for so faithfully filling the first role, and Adrienne Hickey for her forbearance in the second.

And a special thanks to Sourcebooks, Inc., for their commitment to bringing this book to market, and to Peter Lynch for his advocacy and superb editing skills.

Thanks, also, to all the managers—cited and otherwise—who taught me what they knew and shared their wisdom with me. It is you that I acknowledge—and salute—most of all.

Thanks to Genie Carr, who helped shape my scratchy handwriting and garbled dictation into a coherent piece of work. Thanks to Emily Bolton for her quick and accurate transcription. And special thanks to Mary Bolton—without whom there would be no book!

INTRODUCTION

There is a perhaps-apocryphal story about a Broadway producer meeting with an eager young director and playwright. The director-playwright spends forty intense minutes over lunch, breathlessly outlining for the producer a great idea for a play—a play that is sure to be a block-buster. Finally, in exasperation, the producer turns to the young playwright and says, "If you can't write your idea on the back of a business card, then you don't have an idea."

I agree with that Broadway producer. I've always been a reductionist, a simplifier—always looking for that one gem in a bucket of muck, that one irreducible nugget that captures an essential truth about life.

As a child I played football, and I remember the first time I heard a coach say to us, "When the going gets tough, the tough get going." I rolled that sentence around on my tongue and rejoiced at the interplay of those words.

I bumped the sentence up against my understanding of life as an eleven-year-old and found it true. I watched the people with whom I played and found that—when the going in a football game got tough—the tough were the ones who got going. Perhaps I was predisposed from birth to write this book, to gravitate toward pithy sayings that capture an essential truth about life.

As a young political science major in college, I was fascinated by this old saying: "Men and rivers get crooked in the same way—by following the path of least resistance." My limited knowledge of geology demonstrated the truth of this observation for the great rivers of the world, while my knowledge of theology and more complete understanding of history and politics confirmed the statement in the human dimension of life.

It was another aphorism, borne out in the experience of life.

That's what this book is all about: aphorisms and sayings and pithy summing-ups that capture essential truths about life in the managerial world.

Each of the sayings in this book represents a thread woven together into the tapestry we call management. The tapestry—and the information—is *organic*, for we cannot separate the totality of management into individual components. In some ways, it's like asking, "Which organ system do you prefer? Your heart, or your lungs?" Without either, you'd die.

Likewise, the maxims about leadership cannot be separated from the maxims about motivation, and neither of them can be cut off from the maxims related to expectation setting. Each of these maxims is a single thread woven together into the total tapestry we call management.

The maxims cannot be separated in real-world application. For purposes of discussion, however, they must be separated so that we can examine them fully and glean from them the truths they have to offer. And there is much truth here if we can only discern it and appropriate it for proper use.

There are, however, some cautions we must bear in mind, and they are articulated most clearly for us by Mark Twain. Twain once commented, in a statement that is absolutely apropos to the work that we are about to begin, "We should be careful to *get out of an experience only the wisdom that is in it*—and stop there, lest we be like the cat that sits down on a hot stove lid. She will not sit down on a hot stove lid again—and that is well; but also, she will never sit down on a cool one any more."

Much has been made of the increasing complexity of executing business strategies in the twenty-first century. There is a phalanx of consultants out there eager to tell you how difficult it is to manage your business in the face of the increasing pace of change, and how complex are the challenges you confront.

And in some sense, this is true. But it is not *all* of the truth.

Management is now, as it always has been, the judicious application of human, financial, and material resources against the challenges of producing and delivering a product or service in a way that the customers feel well served and the business makes a profit. It is as simple (and as *difficult*) as that.

My own sense is that too much has been made of the complexity of business life. The challenges facing us in the business world are much like the challenge that Sisyphus faced as he tried to push his enormous rock up that steep hill: the task is *difficult* but not *complex*. And as a reductionist—as a simplifier—I find maxims to be useful pointers toward the key (and core) challenges and truths that inform any difficult situation.

Maxims have much to teach us even when they exist in apparent contradiction one to the other. We are told simultaneously, "He who hesitates is lost," and "Fools rush in where angels fear to tread." What are we to make of this; what wisdom can we extract from the apparent clash of these conflicting maxims?

Similarly, in the world of relationships, we are told, "Absence makes the heart grow fonder," and simultaneously that when one is "out of sight, (one is) out of mind." Again, what are we to make of this contradiction? The learning for us, perhaps, is that all things are true *some* of the time, and nothing is true *all* of the time.

Our task—as Mark Twain has so aptly pointed out—is to learn what we can from the maxims before us and not apply them willy-nilly in situations where they have no relevance. Our further challenge—with these maxims and with all of life—is to bump the apparent wisdom contained in the maxim against our life experience and the circumstances we confront, and to extract from that confrontation the wisdom that most fully applies to the circumstances we confront.

With that as our task, let us begin.

VISION AND PLANNING

I once worked for a company where the following story was legend. This company had a number of truck drivers. They drove relatively heavy trucks throughout the Southeast, delivering an automotive after-market product to dealers for resale. This particular incident was reported to have happened in Kentucky.

An excited truck driver called to say that his truck had fallen through a bridge, and was now hanging precariously in the under-supports of that bridge, twenty feet above a scenic waterway. He asked us what he should do.

Our first response was, "How in the world did your truck fall through a bridge?"

His reply? "Well, it turns out that the bridge had a load limit of 10 tons, and my truck weighs 55 tons."

"Didn't you know this?" we responded.

"Oh, no," he replied. "The first I knew of it was when I fell through the bridge."

With our curiosity piqued, we sent a management team

member out to assess the situation. When he got into the county where the incident occurred, he began to drive down the small country road leading to the bridge. He was surprised to see, not far in front of him, a sign. The sign said, "Caution. Scenic covered bridge ahead. Load limit: 10 tons."

On he continued; several miles later he encountered another sign. "Caution. Scenic covered bridge ahead. Nine miles. Load limit: 10 tons." Past that sign he drove, only to encounter another sign. "Caution. Scenic covered bridge ahead. Four miles. Load limit: 10 tons." And yet another sign. "Caution. Scenic covered bridge ahead. Two miles. Load limit: 10 tons." Then another. "Caution. Scenic covered bridge ahead. One mile. Load limit: 10 tons."

When he approached the bridge—the now-bottomless bridge with the truck dangling dangerously above the scenic waterway—a large, orange sign affixed to the covered bridge said, "Caution. Proceed slowly. Load limit: 10 tons."

From this, we derived our own internal maxim: "If you don't read the signs, you'll fall through the bridge."

If You Don't Read the Signs, You'll Fall Through the Bridge

Reading the signs is all about *vision*; it's about climbing all the way up the mast to the crow's nest of your business-ship to get a clear understanding of where you have been and what lies before you. It's about surveying the sea and the horizon a full 360 degrees—looking for both channels of opportunity and dangerous shoals of misdirection.

Vision exists *before* we chart the course. Vision is about understanding the climate and the currents, knowing the abilities and weaknesses of your crew and vessel, and selecting an achievable destination that will yield profits to the ship's owner plus safe passage and fair wages to the crew.

Vision weighs the risks of one route versus another; vision considers the current atmosphere and the competitive ships. And vision ultimately decides: "For this ship, in this port, given these conditions, the best destination is X." Only then are the sailors ready to begin charting their course, planning the safest and fastest route to this destination that accords with their vision.

It's easy to get it backwards; to begin planning before the vision is clear, to confuse tactics with objectives, and to give in to the great American prejudice for action: "Do something wrong, but *do something*!" And it's a mistake that can kill a business.

If we begin to act without a close reading of the environment, clear objectives, and a coherent strategy, we will fail ourselves, our company, and our employees. We will launch products just as consumer demand for them has peaked and is beginning to fall. We will staff up and make tremendous capital expenditures to manufacture a product that is at the tail end of its life cycle, or we will incorrectly discern that there is tremendous market demand for a product that, while still healthy, is beginning to plateau.

Reading the signs gives us knowledge of market growth or stagnation, of technological change or relative stasis, of burgeoning consumer demand or slackening interest in our product.

So one of our key jobs as managers is to read the signs. And it is from the sign reading that we derive our plans, using the signs (economic trends, market share data, consumer surveys, industry analyses) to keep us from falling through the bridge. If we lose sight of the signs, we may wind up managing efficient business operations that are all pointed to a flawed strategy. And that can be disastrous.

Manage the Vision and the Strategy, Not Just the Business Operations

A good friend of mine (a bright and accomplished manager with great passion for his work) once worked for a major regional catalog showroom chain. As you likely know, catalog showrooms have largely disappeared from our economic landscape. They have been buffeted on the one side by big-box toy retailers who took away a substantial share of their business, and have been slammed on the other side by megastore consumer electronics and appliance retailers who took away *that* part of their business.

This manager spoke of the challenges they faced in the catalog showroom business and how they had confronted them. His response was telling. He said, *"We managed the business well; we just didn't manage the strategy."*

There is a wealth of wisdom captured in this statement, and we can learn much from it. My friend spoke to the fact that his company had done a good job of managing the store operations in their showroom.

They built a top-flight warehouse and kept costs down. They distributed products at efficient prices to their stores. They found good locations for their stores, and stocked and staffed them well. They did a great job of managing their business *operations*. Unfortunately, they didn't manage the *strategy* well. The market niche that catalog showrooms had carved out for themselves—a market niche in which they survived and flourished for decades—disappeared. Big-box toy retailers and megastore consumer electronics chains whacked catalog showrooms in these two key product categories. Superstore home centers snatched away the lawn and garden business. Eventually, catalog showrooms were left with the dregs of mid- to low-price jewelry sales and some moderate sporting equipment sales, which didn't leave them enough volume to generate a profit. The showrooms could not see beyond the trees of their operational excellence to the forest of their disappearing market, so *they* disappeared. It's a tragedy, and it's all the more tragic because it did not *have* to happen.

Managers must not only manage their business operations, they must also understand the impact of changing market conditions on the strategy they have articulated. And they must continually ask themselves, "Is the plan we crafted last year consonant with the market conditions we face this year?" If there was ever a call for continuous improvement processes, that call is found in the planning process for businesses in our era of fast-paced change and market evolution. It was a challenge my friend's company could not meet.

In the early stages of the business' demise, several key management members identified the flawed strategy as a major problem with the company. They climbed the crow's nest, surveyed the horizon for a safe place to sail, and identified a likely port of call: the superstore jewelry business.

Their executives asked the key strategic questions: what do we do well? What are our strengths? Which market is underserved? How can we fill it profitably? And the superstore jewelry business—the Toys 'R' Us of jewelry retail—was an unfilled niche. It looked to be safe, profitable sailing.

But the most-senior members of management could not—would not—embrace this change in direction. The admirals vetoed the proposed course, the ship ran aground on the shoals of a disappearing market, and then it sank in a sea of red ink.

It could have turned out differently, but senior management was married to the plan. In the end, no amount of cajoling could get them to sign a separation agreement. It's a pity.

 ## A Plan Is Not a Straitjacket—Build Flex into Your Plan

Have you ever seen a straitjacket? They are made of heavy canvas. The wearer steps into it "backward," and it is secured down the back, with fasteners conveniently out of reach of the wearer. But that's only the beginning.

The sleeves of the straitjacket are then crossed across the body of the wearer and tied behind the wearer's back. It is—quite literally—impossible to move your upper body when wearing one. Affixed too tightly, they even make it difficult to breathe.

Yet many businesspeople treat their business plan like a straitjacket. It's written, it's typed, it's published, and it's bound. And it becomes sacrosanct. A plan should be a *guide* and *only* a guide.

A plan is a snapshot, taken at a moment in time, of the path forward that looks most attractive to a company at that moment in time. Circumstances change. Competitors grow or weaken. Markets open, fads fade, and consumers are bewitched by the next "most attractive" thing. If we are so constrained by our plan that we cannot see the changes going on in the market, we are as condemned to fail as people who never planned at all.

So remember: a plan is not a straitjacket. Build flex into your plan. That being said, a countervailing point obtains as well.

A Business Is Not a Restaurant—Avoid "Strategy du Jour"

If it is fatal to get a death grip on a strategy and never let go, it can be equally deadly to operate a business on the "strategy du jour" model. I once worked with a client who seemed to embrace this strategy, and it was the most bewildering experience of my life.

The company's strategy changed so often—and was communicated so poorly—that sometimes field operations people were *two or three strategies behind.* Their strategies changed so often that, when holding a four o'clock meeting, we had to check to make sure the company was still on the strategy articulated at the nine o'clock in the morning meeting.

Are we going to sell direct-to-consumer or use a distributor network? Go to distributors through manufacturer's reps or a dedicated company sales force? Own our manufacturing or outsource it? Be a technical innovator or a fast follower?

Companies can and do succeed by selecting either of the options in these pairs. But they rarely succeed by changing rapidly and repeatedly from one to the other.

In many ways, this company was like a child with hyperactivity/attention deficit disorder. The company changed strategies and directions so often that it was hard to focus on any topic or goal long enough to achieve it. Projects were started with great enthusiasm then stopped abruptly. Four months later, they were restarted. But this time the energy and passion level was diminished—sapped by the constant to-ing and fro-ing of the strategy du jour management style.

The downside of this approach to management is multifold:

- ➷ IT PERPLEXES THE EMPLOYEES. They are never at all sure what it is they are supposed to be trying to accomplish *today*, under *this plan, this time around*.

- ➷ IT CONFUSES THE CUSTOMERS, who are never quite sure what this company stands for *this* week.

- ➷ IT BEWILDERS WALL STREET, which has a lot on its mind anyway and is completely unable to fathom what a company is about when it changes strategy more than biennially.

Why would a company change strategies so often? What drives this behavior? Sometimes it's the absence of a decisive, visionary leader at the apex of the organizational pyramid. Sometimes it's the presence of two competing leaders—leaders who have divergent views about where the company ought to go. Most often, though, companies do the strategy shuffle because they seek the lone, perfect, bulletproof strategy for their industry.

 ## Give It Up! There Is No Lone, Perfect Strategy

What's the best way to make money in the automobile business? Should you produce lots of high quality cars and sell them to the mass market like Toyota? Or should you produce relatively fewer cars—still high quality, of course— and target a premium demographic as Mercedes has done?

What about the tool business? Does it make more sense to sell through mass retailers and home centers like Stanley Tool Works? Or should you market through independent distributors as Snap-On Tools has done?

Who's right? Both of them are right. Each of these companies, while pursuing a strategy vastly different than its paired competition, has been successful. There is no one perfect, all-purpose, bulletproof strategy. So the search for a perfect strategy is pointless; it merely consumes time that could better be spent elsewhere. If your strategy is even close, and if your people buy that strategy and embrace it passionately, that's good enough.

Eighty Percent Strategy Executed with 100 Percent Commitment Always Beats 100 Percent Strategy Executed with 80 Percent Commitment

"Whether you think you can—or whether you think you can't—either way you're right!" I don't remember the first person who said this to me; it was many, many years ago. And it's true—commitment and belief are two of the key drivers to any strategy's success.

So how do we get this level of commitment? Do we demand it? Or can we engender it? There's an old saying that is apropos here: "You can *force compliance*; you have to *earn commitment.*"

And we earn commitment by involving the employees—to the extent appropriate—in the creation of the goals.

Input Raises Buy-In

It is a management truth that the people closest to the work generally have the best idea about how the work should be done. Why not? They live it every day. Yet managers regularly ignore the insights and opinions of their followers as they develop strategic vision and operating plans for their organizations. That's too bad, because a little bit of input will produce a quantum increase in (1) the employee's commitment to the strategy and the plan, and (2) the quality of the plan itself.

People like to give input. Input increases the likelihood of their commitment.

Think about the sales world; there's even a sales technique driven solely by this observation. In *closing on a minor point*, the salesperson asks the customer, "Would you prefer that appliance in stainless steel or classic white?" The opportunity to have input heightens the likelihood that the customer will buy the appliance at all.

Or reflect for a moment on the world of parenting. A tired six-year-old is approaching bedtime. Two tasks remain before he can go to bed: taking a bath and picking up his room. The parent could dictate what gets done first, with predictable results. Or, the parent could ask for the child's input: "What would you like to do first, pick up your room or take a bath?" And the buy-in would likely be higher, and the protest moderated.

Input raises buy-in. If you truly and authentically seek 100 percent commitment to your strategy, the easiest way to engender that commitment is to involve the people who will execute the strategy in its creation.

If You Don't Know Where You're Going, You'll Probably End Up Somewhere Else

Defining a cogent business vision and articulating the objectives, strategies, and tactics to support this vision: this is the *foundational* task of managers.

"We must ask ourselves," Abraham Lincoln once said, "from whence we have come and whither we are tending." And—I might add—if whither we are tending is where we intended to tend. We can only make assessments about what and how we are doing if we know what (and how) we intended to do. *We must know where we are going.*

So our job is to help the organization develop a vision—an understanding of what it stands for and wants to become. From that vision we shake out the key objectives—the specific goals that will help flesh out the vision.

It is where we are going—our vision and goals—that drive everything else, as this excerpt from Lewis Carroll's *Alice in Wonderland* illustrates. In the story, Alice encounters the Cheshire Puss, and a conversation ensues.

"Cheshire Puss,"…said Alice, "would you tell me, please, which way I ought to go from here?"

"That depends a good deal on where you want to get to," said the Cat.

"I don't much care where—" said Alice.

"Then it doesn't matter which way you go," said the Cat.

So we must know where we're going as we begin to plan. And knowing where—at least conceptually—is not enough. We need details.

If You Fail to Plan, Then Plan to Fail—Prior Planning Prevents Poor Performance

Our final maxims present us with two sides of the same truth. Planning does not guarantee success. The absence of planning virtually guarantees failure.

Shape that vision. Develop those objectives. Plan to as fine a level of detail as will work in your business, remembering that your plan is a blueprint, not a straitjacket.

Planning. It's critical to you and your company. Remember, if you don't know where you're going, you'll probably end up somewhere else.[1]

MAXIMS ON VISION AND PLANNING

If you don't read the signs, you'll fall through the bridge.

Manage the vision and strategy, not just the business operations.

A plan is not a straitjacket—build flex into your plan.

A business is not a restaurant—avoid strategy du jour.

Give it up! There is no lone, perfect strategy.

Eighty percent strategy executed with 100 percent commitment always beats 100 percent strategy executed with 80 percent commitment.

Input raises buy-in.

If you don't know where you're going, you'll probably end up somewhere else.

If you fail to plan, then plan to fail—prior planning prevents poor performance.

QUESTIONS FOR REFLECTION

1. When was a time in your business or personal life where you missed the "signs"? How did you "fall through the bridge"?

2. What examples can you think of where someone managed the business *operations* but mismanaged

the business *vision* and *strategy*? What were the results?

3. Why do you think companies get straitjacketed in their plans? What could be done to avoid this?

4. "If you don't know where you're going, you'll probably end up somewhere else." What evidence have you seen to validate this statement? In you own life? In your workplace? Elsewhere?

CHALLENGE FOR APPLICATION

How can you—in the planning/visioning you do in your organization—elicit input to engender buy-in? What would work best? Where will you start?

2

MOTIVATION

There's been more garbage written about motivation than about any other subject in the history of the world—except perhaps love and sex. This is because motivation is a lot like love and sex: it's all quicksilver, elusive, and hard to pin down. Almost anything you say about motivation is true—some of the time—and very little of it is true all of the time. That's why there's so much garbage out there.

In truth, motivation is really pretty simple. It boils down to three things:

1. No one can motivate anyone to do anything.

2. We *can* create circumstances in which people motivate themselves.

3. You've got to walk the talk.

No One Can Motivate Anyone to Do Anything

This adage reminds me of a time when I was a young, green manager, just beginning to try my hand at motivating large groups of people. My boss called me into his office and said, "Son, we're having a sales meeting! I want you to go get me some motivational films!!" So, dutiful kid that I was, off to the library I went to get some motivational films.

The more I watched those films, the more nauseated I became. Here was a golly-gee-whiz instructor learning to shoot an aspirin out of the air with a pellet gun, all in the name of communicating the notion that you *can* do it, if you'll only *try*.

In another of the films, a well-known retired coach drew dozens of parallels from the world of athletics. He exhorted the audience to subordinate their *individual* aspirations to the good of the *team*, because there is no letter "I" in the word "team."

The ideas were all well and good. But how? How exactly do we engender motivation? What do we do to help our followers overcome inertia, fear, and fatigue to deliver on-purpose, productive behavior that helps both them and their organization achieve specific objectives?

I eventually realized that motivation doesn't come out of film cans. It comes from people's heads and hearts. And we can't get into their heads and hearts—we are forever wholly other, in an orbit totally outside them. So we cannot ever motivate anyone to do anything—it has to come from inside them. But we *can* create an environment in which others motivate themselves. And that brings us to point two.

We *Can* Create Circumstances in Which People Motivate Themselves

In the mid-1970s, I managed a branch bank for one of North Carolina's major financial institutions. One bright winter day, two robbers burst into the bank. One aimed a sawed-off, twelve-gauge shotgun directly at my face and screamed, "Give me all of your money!"

Did he get inside my head? No—he wasn't a psychiatrist. Did he get inside my heart? No—he was neither my cardiologist nor my lover. Did he create a circumstance in which I motivated myself? Yes indeed. Did he get the money? Absolutely!

An extreme illustration, perhaps. But let's look at it a little deeper to see what we can learn. Our robber succeeded by creating *goal alignment*. That is, he helped me see that I could get what I wanted (keeping my youthful countenance intact) by giving him what he wanted (all of the money). We struck a bargain, and both walked (actually, he ran) away happy.

Our robber-motivator answered a fundamental question by the use of his shotgun as a visual aid. He answered the what's-in-it-for-me question and showed me the benefits if I complied with his request. And his reward for me (life) was worth his requirement ("Give me all of the money").

Let's look now at the third of our introductory precepts.

You've Got to Walk the Talk

This is a sophomoric phrase. It's old and it's trite. It's also true. Managers have to demonstrate to their followers that they believe, support, and embrace everything that they ask their followers to do.

Assume, for instance, that coming in early and leaving late is one of your company's big values. But you, personally, come in at nine o'clock and leave at three. It won't take your employees long to realize that you are not committed to this corporate standard in any meaningful way. And the absence of your personal commitment will quickly translate to a diminishment of their personal commitment as well, and a concurrent absence of their brains, if not their actual bodies, from eight to nine and from three to five.

In many ways, this example is the converse of precept two. By demonstrating no personal commitment to the goal, you, as manager, have created an environment in which employees *de*-motivate themselves. Performance plummets. The whole company loses. What's the antidote? WII-FM! The world's most powerful radio station (see Figure 2-1).

Broadcast on Radio Station WII-FM

WII-FM is the world's most powerful radio station. It broadcasts around the clock, around the world, twenty-four hours a day. We first met this concept in the bank robber story. WII-FM (our radio station call letters) stands for *W*hat's *I*n *I*t *F*or *M*e.

The altruists among us often object to this model. "But what about self-sacrifice?" they say. "What about Mother Teresa? What about soldiers who throw themselves on hand grenades to save their unit?" These are all good questions, and we will explore them in more detail as we work.

WII-FM

FIGURE 2-1

The questions, however, do not point out any inherent flaw in the model. It's the one that leads us to floss (WII-FM? Healthy teeth), jog (WII-FM? Health and longevity), and pray (WII-FM? A connection with the immanent-yet-transcendent Other).

There are abuses of WII-FM, and we've all seen them in acquisitive, self-absorbed me-ism. But that's not the fault of the model. Let's look at the immediate applicability of the model to the world of business and management.

Why did you buy your last car? Price? Style? Necessity? There's your WII-FM. How did you choose the dealer? Price? Friendship? Proximity? Service excellence? There's your WII-FM. Every day, all day long, we make choices that answer this question and help us select from a bewildering array of options. And the model applies to motivation as well as to purchase choices.

Why do you work where you do? Compensation? Benefits? Opportunity? There's your WII-FM! Why did you turn down the last job you turned down? Too much risk? Too much work? Too much time away? There's your WII-FM! We all have 'em, all the time, about everything.

And so do our employees, which brings us to a key maxim for motivation.

If You *Listen* Long Enough, People Will Tell You What Motivates Them

Nobody listens anymore.

All day we are bombarded with messages. We wake up to a clock radio, eat breakfast in front of the television, and drive to work listening to satellite radio or an iPod. We've got cell phones, iPhones, and BlackBerries. Our laptops ping every time a new email hits the inbox. All day long, we are assaulted by a barrage of messages. But we never get *listened to*, which is too bad.

People are crying to be—dying to be—heard. And, as managers, if we'll just stop and listen, they will tell us what matters to them. They will tell us what motivates them. And it's our job to respond in a way that is faithful to what they say they need, and to our role in the corporation. Listening—and responding out of what you hear—is one of the single greatest motivators at a manager's disposal. Let me give you an example.

I once worked with a fellow—we'll call him Don—who was smart as a whip. Don was from the Southeast, grew up poor, went to college, and washed out. He got a job and learned a lot. For the next fifteen years, he moved up to progressively more responsible positions and was well-regarded in his industry.

Don worked for me, and it took me a while to learn to shut up and listen so that I could manage and motivate him well. Two things made Don go: the trappings of power and face time with his boss. Those aren't my hot buttons, and I didn't recognize them immediately as key motivators.

Trappings of power mattered to Don. He'd count the ceiling tiles in his office, convert the number to square feet, and compare his office size to that of his peers. If his office was "too small" for his status, he'd sulk.

Since these things don't matter to me, it took me a long time to get it. I simply don't care about the trappings of power as long as the phone works, there's decent light, and the air-conditioning will keep it cold enough to kill hogs. I'm happy sitting on a Coke crate and working off a folding table. But I'm not Don.

And it's not my job to change Don into me. It's my job to manage him as he is. Once I figured out what Don needed—it was part of who he was—I acknowledged it and got him what he needed. He had a big desk, a beautiful walnut credenza, and a blazing-fast computer with all the bells and whistles. I was halfway to having a great employee. But *only* halfway.

The other thing Don needed was face time with me. He needed affirmation. He needed reassurance. He wanted to hear it said that he wasn't the poor child he grew up as, or the dumb nineteen-year-old who flunked out of college. It took me even longer to hear this. Don was telling me how to motivate him, but I wouldn't listen.

I like to go to work early—really early. I've always said you can get more done between five and eight than you can between eight and five. So in I'd go. And I'd be just shoveling—digging out from under the pile on my desk. (*It's only 7:10. If I really hurry, I can get it all done by eight.*) And in walks Don.

Damn, I think. "Hi," I say. And Don launches into a long explanation of a project he has just done for me— one he wants to review right now. He pulls out graphs and flowcharts, readying himself for what I fear will be an interminable conversation. Neophyte that I am, I'm *too busy working to be a good manager.* So I give him lip service and shoo him down the hall. His shoulders slump as he slouches dejectedly out the door.

Whose fault was this? Mine! Don has told me how to motivate him. He wants face time with his boss. And I need to figure out how to deliver what motivates him, or find him a manager who will.

People Come in Two Types: Carrot People and Stick People

"Carrot people"—what a peculiar figure of speech! We all know what a "stick" person is, but what's a "carrot" person?

Actually, a stick person—in this context, anyhow—is not a crude drawing. This adage refers to the fact that some people are motivated by the prospect of rewards (carrots) while others only work to avoid consequences (sticks).

One reason we *listen* to people is to uncover whether they respond better to the prospect of eating carrots or avoiding the prospect of being whacked by a stick. And one reason we observe people is to see if *what they said is how they live.*

As important as listening is, it's not the only window into the reality of an employee's motivational profile. Sometimes, in fact, people will not give voice to their most powerful motivators. Instead, they talk about motivators that they think are more socially acceptable.

Money is perhaps the most concrete example of an oft-voiced, socially acceptable motivator. If you ask a group of disgruntled workers what would make them happy, money will inevitably top the list. However, if you give them a 10 percent raise and check back in three months, they will likely still be disgruntled. Why? Because money wasn't the whole—or perhaps even the *main*—issue. Money was just the easiest to quantify and articulate of the multiple motivators operating in the situation.

Perhaps these employees felt taken for granted—left unrecognized by the supervisors for whom they work so hard. What they really needed was recognition. But few employees can look a supervisor in the eye and say, "Hey, Boss, I need a hug!" So they talk about money, and we give raises. Yet everyone is surprised when the level of discontent does not go down.

Yes, we need to listen, because listening is one way to determine what motivates people. And we also need to *watch*, to *observe*, to *pay attention* to what our employees value, because this can be even more powerful.

If You *Watch* Long Enough, People Will Show You How to Motivate Them

Watching is at least as effective as listening in ferreting out an employee's key motivators. Students of body language tell us it is easier to read a person's true response from body language than from words. Why? Because my mouth can say, "Fine," when my eyes and countenance reflect disappointment. And the eyes and countenance are the most apt to be truthful.

Similarly, employees communicate what most matters to them by where they put their time and resources. They may spend hours and hours with their family or their favorite sport or their hobby. If they do, you can be reasonably assured that free time for these activities would be a key motivator.

I once worked with a client who learned this lesson the hard way.

My client was a hugely successful automobile dealer with many lines and multiple locations. He bought a sleepy, cob-webbed domestic car dealership and began to jump-start it back to life. One of the first things he noticed was the slow pace of work in the service department of his new dealership. So that's where he began his work.

At another of his dealerships, his highest-paid service technician had made $65,000-plus the previous year—and this was in the late 1980s. My friend sat his new service people down and said, "I've reviewed the records and see that most of you made $25,000 to $35,000 last year. You can do much better than that now. We're gonna open early and stay open late. I'm gonna invest in equipment and tools. We will serve our customers well. And the best of you can easily make $50,000-plus in the next twelve months. All it requires from you is a commitment to do good work faster, to work harder and smarter than you ever have. Now let's go get 'em!" And with that exhortation, he sent them back to work.

Ninety days later, nothing had changed. The pace was still slow. The average technician was making $2,200 a month. So my friend called one of the leaders from his shop crew. He reviewed the spiel from three months before and noted the unchanged pace of work in the shop. Then he stopped, looked his employee in the eye, and queried, "So what's the deal? Don't people want to make $50,000?"

And what he heard was something he could have observed had he only watched for the key motivators of his team.

"Look," the employee began. "You're a nice young fellow. I want you to succeed. But you don't understand. I've got a paid-for house on fifteen acres out in the country. I've got a truck and a fishin' boat. My garage has two freezers full of wild game I've killed and dressed. I don't want to make

$50,000 a year. I want three months off a year to go huntin' and fishin'. That's what I want. That's what trips my trigger!"

And now my friend *knew*. He knew how to motivate this employee; he had found the reward that fired this employee's rocket. It wasn't money—it was *time*. That was the carrot that would pull optimal response from this employee. Had my friend watched, he would have known it sooner. It was clear from this employee's behavior that time off was his great love.

So we watch and we listen—always trying to identify the carrot that pulls high performance from our teammates. Sometimes it is money or time off or recognition or status. It's not our job to judge 'em or even to change 'em. It's just our job to uncover the motivators and make them available.

But what do we do when there is no apparent carrot—when watching and listening still yield no clues to what will motivate an individual? Sometimes we change tactics.

You Can Waste A Lot of Time Feeding Carrots to Stick People

In the early 1980s, I was promoted to a job that was a lot bigger than I was. I had over two hundred employees; I was only thirty-two. Some of the people who worked for me were older than my father; some of them had been working since before I was born.

I was a one-trick pony; the only thing I knew how to do was wave the flag, cheerlead, pat people on the fanny, and holler, "Rah-rah." Fortunately, I followed a guy who was widely perceived as insensitive and dictatorial, so it wasn't hard to be thought a better manager than he was.

I began to practice participatory management. I got the employees' input on what we should do, and we talked about how we could go to market better. At the same time, we re-shaped the organization to give many members of the team raises and promotions. When I took the job, 30 percent of the people were working. I looked around after about six months, and 80 percent of them were working.

"I'm a genius!" I thought. But I needed them *all* to work. So I gave another round of raises and promotions and job title changes. In another six months, I looked around and 82 percent of them were working.

Clearly, anybody who was going to be motivated by cheerleading and fanny-patting and new titles and the excitement I tried to engender was motivated in the first wave. And now I was out of titles and out of money and out of time—I was out of *carrots*. And 18 percent of the people still weren't working.

There were two people on the team that clearly weren't going to make it. So I got on a plane and flew to the Midwest and dismissed one of them. And I got on another plane and flew to the Northeast and invited a second one to pursue employment opportunities with other corporations. I came home, looked around, and guess what: *everybody* was working. They realized I had a *stick* to complement my carrots. You've likely got some idea what happened when news of the first dismissal began to circulate on the company grapevine. Folks called each other on the phone and said, "Damn! That young college boy can fire people, too! In fact, I hear he's on the way to your place next!"

For people who are motivated by carrots, you dangle carrots in front of them, promise them good things, and make good things happen to and for them. They will respond in ways that astound even themselves—assuming you have listened and are offering them carrots they really want.

However, some people don't like carrots. They also do not like to be hit. Some people *work to embrace pleasure*, and other people *work to avoid pain*. Our job is to figure out who is who and offer them the thing that gets them off their butts the fastest. And sometimes a little fear is not a bad thing.

I believe that—as a matter of principle—we should offer carrots first. A manager's obligation is to assume in the beginning that people are of good intent and want to do a good job. To assume—in other words—that all employees are "carrot" people. The price of being a manager is that you occasionally waste time and money on the front end because not all employees are carrot people. Still, it's the best approach to take; it honors the dignity of your employees.

After the first go-round, you see who hasn't responded. You make sure you were clear in what you communicated to them. You check to make sure you listened well and watched closely to identify their key motivators. You ensure that the carrots you *offered* were carrots they *liked*. And—if they are still not responding—you can begin to assume that they are stick people, motivated more by fear of pain than by pursuit of pleasure. So you ratchet up the fear. You're not mad at them, you're just doing your job: creating a circumstance in which they can motivate themselves.

If you watch people—watch how they work, listen to them as they talk about the things they value and how they live their lives—they will tell you whether they are carrot or stick people. And we can incorporate that knowledge as we apply the motivational model[1] shown in Figure 2-2.

Let's dissect this motivational model step by step, beginning at point A with the earliest question: "If I try, can I do it?" This question informs all attempts at motivation, because when given a meaningful task they don't feel able to do, most people will not try, regardless of the payoffs or the consequences (the carrots or the sticks, in the language we have been using).

So our first job as motivators is to make sure we have properly matched the task to the person—that we have selected well, trained appropriately, and equipped properly. Beyond these factors, we must also build confidence so the employees *believe* in their ability to actually *do* it.

Once we have properly matched an employee with a task the employee can do, we are ready to move fully into the carrot/stick motivation mode.

At point B in the model, shown in Figure 2-2, we see our employee pleading with us to broadcast the WII-FM to them. "What's in it for me?" they ask. If I do it, will I be rewarded—will I get a carrot? If I don't do it, will I feel consequences—will that stout stick swat me on my thick hide?

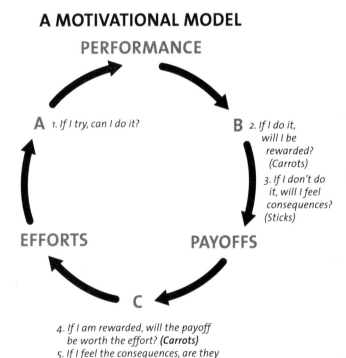

A MOTIVATIONAL MODEL

PERFORMANCE

A *1. If I try, can I do it?*

B *2. If I do it, will I be rewarded? (Carrots)*

3. If I don't do it, will I feel consequences? (Sticks)

EFFORTS

PAYOFFS

C

4. If I am rewarded, will the payoff be worth the effort? ***(Carrots)***

5. If I feel the consequences, are they severe enought to avoid? ***(Sticks)***

FIGURE 2-2

Point B is where we bring into play the learning we have gleaned from *listening* and *watching* for key motivators. And the motivators don't always have to be carrots, either. We tend to judge those who are stick-motivated, but the truth is that we are all a meld of carrot-driven and stick-driven.

Taxes and speed limits help point out the stick component of motivation in even the most highly motivated among us. Think for a moment about your last trip of any distance on our interstate highways. What was the speed limit? Sixty-five? How fast did you go? Seventy? Seventy-five? Eighty? Why didn't you go 100 miles per hour? You certainly would have gotten to your destination faster!

Likely you didn't go 100 miles per hour for one of three key reasons:

1. You feared getting a ticket, which would slow you down and cost you money.

2. You feared damaging your car, or getting killed, which would really slow you down and cost you money.

3. You feared a confrontation ("You lunatic!") with your spouse or passenger, which would cost you respect and make you look bad.

There was no real "carrot" for obeying the speed limit. You could feel good about yourself for being a law-abiding citizen, but so what? No one else was doing it! No one else was walking the talk. In truth, it is mostly sticks that determine the pace at which any one of us drives.

Likewise, if you owed Uncle Sam money, when did you mail your tax return and your check? April 15? Why didn't you mail it March 1 and feel like a good citizen who had forgone a month-and-a-half of interest on his funds? Isn't that carrot enough—the heartfelt (if unexpressed) gratitude of the IRS?

Conversely, why didn't you just withhold payment altogether? After all, the government has been withholding from you for years. Didn't want to get that IRS audit notice, did you? That's stick enough for us all!

Once we have selected the right person and matched them to a task, we then offer carrots and sticks as appropriate. The fundamental crunch-point of motivation is ensuring that the *carrots we offer are ones the employee wants*, and the *sticks we hold are ones the employee fears*.

My mother used to say to me, "I'm going to spank you." I'd been spanked by her; it didn't hurt. So this stick didn't much motivate me. Then she would add this caboose to that sentence: "And if I have to spank you, I'm going to tell your father when he comes home from work, and *he'll* spank you, too."

Well…I'd been spanked by him, too, and *that* was worth avoiding. So, she provided a motivational "stick" that helped me motivate myself to behave, and she got the results she sought. I shaped up to avoid Daddy's discipline.

When we speak of carrot people, they are the ones whose impetus to act comes primarily from Questions 2 and 4 (see Figure 2-2). When we speak of stick people, their impetus to act comes largely from Questions 3 and 5 (see Figure 2-2). Neither is better or worse, but it helps to know what you are working with as you manage someone.

As we've discussed, each person is a blend of carrot and stick motivation. Most of us obey speed-limit signs and pay taxes out of Questions 3 and 5—a clear stick model. Most of us love our pets and families out of 2 and 4—the reward of a loving smile being worth amazing sacrifice.

The total number of motivators in the world is surprisingly small—reflecting the universal nature of motivation. There are perhaps twenty carrot motivators, and a like number of stick motivators. As you review the lists in Figures 2-3 (carrots)[2] and 2-4 (sticks)[3] you'll likely find the key motivators that float your boat.

Not all motivators work all the time for anyone, and we often find ourselves involved in trade-offs when assessing motivation. For example, you may be tremendously motivated to learn a new skill that uses cutting-edge technology (a carrot from the list in Figure 2-3). In the short term, learning the skill will cost you time and generate hassles (a stick from the list in Figure 2-4). But you learn it anyway because you perceive the long-term benefit to be worth the short-term cost.

Sometimes, the motivator for a particular action can be hard to discern unless we look carefully and suspend our own values and motivational profile.

What motivated Mother Teresa to serve the dying poor in India? Was it money? Was it a chance to work less—to kick back and coast? Was it the commodious accommodations or the luxurious clothing? Was it even a Nobel Peace Prize?

REWARDS / CARROTS

• Make more money	• Spend less money	• Save more
• Work fewer hours	• Play more	• Have more time off
• Feel heard	• Have fewer hassles	• Be appreciated
• Security	• Safety	• Work with people I like
• Autonomy (leave me alone!)	• Be part of a winning team	• Learn something new
• Have fun!	• Use new technology	• Do something that matters/ make a difference
• Be all I can be	• Have more responsibility	• Be "in the know"
• Serve some sort of higher order (e.g., God)/goal		
• Look good to any or all of these groups:		

· self	· spouse
· friends	· family
· suppliers	· customers
· employees/subordinates	· peers/co-workers
· boss	· community

Figure 2-3

The answer to this question can be found in a now-legendary story about Mother Teresa. In a lengthy interview with Mother Teresa, a reporter commented, "I would not do what you do for a million dollars!"

Mother Teresa responded, "Neither would I."

If we look at Figure 2-3, we can hazard a guess at the motivators driving Mother Teresa's work: serving God/a higher-order goal, being all she could be, doing something she liked. Clearly she was highly motivated—she worked long hours for many years at very low pay. Her motivators were different from the ones that often come to mind when we think about our typical employee. And it's important to remember this, because those motivators may also motivate the people with whom *we* work.

Here's another example: what motivates Greenpeace members to board small Zodiac rafts and ride them into the path of nuclear-powered warships? Do they do it because they like being nearly drowned in the ship's wake? Do they enjoy seeing the inside of every civilian and Navy jail in the ports they picket? Some may, but I'm betting they do this dangerous work in the name of one of the carrots that fueled Mother Teresa—serving the human good.

We may or may not agree with the key motivators that energize our followers. But whether we agree with—and share—their worldview is inconsequential. It's our job to discern the motivators that pull maximum, on-purpose behavior from our team and offer up those motivators

CONSEQUENCES / STICKS

· Make less money	· Spend more money	· Save less
· Work more hours	· Play less	· Have no time off
· Not feel heard	· Have more hassles	· Not be appreciated
· Lack of security	· Lack of safety	· Work with people I dislike
· No autonomy	· Be part of a losing team	· Never get to learn something new
· Have no fun	· Use old technology	· Do something that doesn't matter

· Feel pain

· Not be able to serve some sort of higher order (e.g. God)/goal

· Look bad to any or all of these groups:

· self	· spouse
· friends	· family
· suppliers	· customers
· employees/subordinates	· peers/coworkers
· boss	· community

FIGURE 2-4

whenever we are able. We must offer up the carrots or the sticks that best help our followers do a good job for themselves and for their organization.

Each of the motivational factors can be turned inside out. That is to say, "Make more money," (a carrot motivator) can become, "Make less money" (a stick motivator). However, we cannot make these transitions willy-nilly. For example, most people don't do things to lose security; security is a carrot motivator, but insecurity is not a stick motivator. What motivates thirteen-year-old boys to walk across the girders of unfinished buildings is not that they like insecurity but that they like the accolades of their peers standing on the ground cheering. So the true motivator here is not a stick (absence of security), but a carrot (cheering throngs, looking good).

The Managerial Golden Rule: Do Unto Others *as They Would Like to Be Done Unto!*

We're all familiar with the Golden Rule: "Do unto others as you would have them do unto you." It has been with us since kindergarten, both in our secular world and in the great streams of religious thought. And it captures a truth that, if lived out, could make life better for all of us.

The Golden Rule has been co-opted, too, hammered into different forms that capture a more jaundiced view of life. The Monetary Golden Rule ("Them that's got the money makes the rules") captures a widely held view in our society. And the Golden Rule for Cynics ("Do unto others before they do unto you") is often cited in the world of buying and selling.

In motivating others, it is the Managerial Golden Rule ("Do unto others *as they would like to be done unto*") that can inform our work. It pulls together all the threads we have talked about and weaves them into a coherent tapestry. Our job as managers is to listen and observe those we manage, so we know how "they would like to be done unto."

For our followers who are carrot people, we watch and listen and dangle before them the items from Figure 2-3 that produce the best results—the ones most germane to their motivational profile.

For our followers who are—for whatever reason—stick people, we revert to the list in Figure 2-4. We make them aware that failure to perform will eventuate into consequences, into the sticks that they most want to avoid.

In both cases, our willingness to "do unto others as they would like to be done unto" allows us to pull the very best performance from them. We find out what it takes to get them to do their best work, and then we serve them, the organization, and ourselves by providing the circumstances that deliver the appropriate carrot or stick.

With the Managerial Golden Rule, we offer people what they most want within the deepest core of their being in return for what *we* need, which is productive and on-target contributions toward our business objectives and goals. We create goal alignment, and everyone wins.

The essence of our discussion—and the summing up of our chapter—is presented in Figure 2-5—The Motivational Charter.

And that's all there is to motivation.

MOTIVATIONAL CHARTER

EMPLOYEES
ARE MOTIVATED WHEN

They believe that if they try *(Effort)*
they will succeed *(Performance)*
and be rewarded *(Payoff)*

and

They believe that if they do not succeed *(No Performance)*
they will feel consequences *(Payoff)*,
and the consequences will be severe enough to avoid.

FIGURE 2-5

⟜ MAXIMS FOR MOTIVATION ⟜

No one can motivate anyone to do anything.

We *can* create circumstances in which people motivate themselves.

You've got to walk the talk.

Broadcast on radio station WII-FM.

If you *listen* long enough, people will tell you what motivates them.

People come in two types: carrot people and stick people.

If you *watch* long enough, people will show you how to motivate them.

You can waste a lot of time feeding carrots to stick people.

The Managerial Golden Rule: "Do unto others *as they would like to be done unto!*"

QUESTIONS FOR REFLECTION

1. What is your gut-level response to WII-FM? Do you believe it is the world's most powerful radio station? Why or why not?

2. When in your own managerial life have you failed to pick up cues about a person's key motivators? What happened?

3. Have you ever tried to motivate a "stick" person with "carrots"? What happened?

4. Have you ever worked for someone who did not "walk the talk"? What impact did this have on your motivation?

CHALLENGE FOR APPLICATION

Think about a current situation where you have an employee who is not performing to the level you expect. If they try, can they do what you are asking of them? (Point A on Figure 2-2.) If the answer is yes, then how can you create circumstances in which they motivate themselves? What carrots/sticks apply? How can you *do unto this employee as he would like to be done unto*?

3

EXPECTATIONS

👍 Paint a Clear Picture of the Target

If motivation is the most *over*taught subject in business management, setting precise expectations (painting a clear picture of the target) is the most *under*taught.

One reason this topic is undertaught is that most people don't clearly understand it—they don't have a clear picture of the target themselves. Managers often don't paint a clear picture of the target because *they don't know precisely what they want as an outcome*. In the end, this causes them a great deal of pain and suffering. It also causes their employees a great deal of frustration and re-work.

An example: I'm sitting happily in my office, working away as a manager for a major international consumer packaged goods company. My director sticks his head in the door and says, "Say, Frank, I've got a four o'clock meeting with our vice president. Could you work me up a sales forecast for next year?" And off he heads down the hall to another meeting.

I begin work. Does he want unit or dollar volume? I give him both to be safe. In aggregate or by region? Region seems safer, so I provide that with an added total column to cover the "aggregate" base. What time period, I wonder. Weekly? Quarterly? Annually? I provide weekly forecasts, with quarterly and annual totals.

The whole process consumes hours, and I slide in the door just as he's heading for his meeting and thrust a thick sheaf of still-warm-from-the-printer pages into his hand.

"What's this?" he asks quizzically. "Oh, the forecast. Gosh, you didn't have to go to so much trouble. All I needed was an aggregate annual national dollar volume number."

I stifle my kill instinct and grumble my way back to the break room, where I wash down four Rolaids with a tumbler of Maalox. Frustration! Re-work the forecast? How about homicide?

I Can't Hit a Target I Can't See

All businesses would operate better if managers knew that their employees were looking at them with this thought in their heads all the time: "I can't hit a target I can't see."

That is, "What is it, *precisely*, that you want me to do?"

Here's an example: every day we leave the office at 11:55 to go somewhere to eat. Let's say we go to Burgher Joynt, where the well-trained counter person says to us, "Welcome to Burgher Joynt. May I take your order?"

Suppose you look at her and say, "Yes. I'd like lunch."

What's going to happen in this scenario? You've told her what you want: lunch. But that's all you've told her. There are several outcomes you are apt to encounter, none of which will satisfy you.

The dense employee will stare at you blankly, then shuffle off to get the manager. She knows she can't hit a target she can't see.

The lazy employee will give you the closest item on the warming tray, and that's not likely what you want. It's probably some item like a filet-of-fish sandwich—not the "A" ticket item in any Burgher Joynt.

The person who's the most customer-focused is going to delve deeply into her brain, coming up with the thing that *she* likes best. So you get what *she* likes, not what *you* like.

But the worst possible outcome will be the employee who's just been approached by the manager—a manager who said, "Push these Big Burghers. They're seventeen minutes old, and if they get three minutes older, we'll have to throw 'em away." So you get a seventeen-minute-old Big Burgher with coagulated grease congealed in the lettuce. And you get it because you didn't paint a clear picture of the target.

Veterans of the fast-food wars know that the best way to get a good meal at any quick-service Burgher restaurant is to walk in and say, "I'd like a Big Burgher, please. Hold the sauce, double the onions, no ketchup." What this means is that you get a grill order (after a deep sigh and an eye-rolling expression from the counter person, who then asks you to step aside, *please*, to wait for your order).

But when it's all said and done, *you get* what *you wanted*, which was hot food, prepared fresh for you. And the only way you got it was to paint for the counter person a clear picture of the target.

So it goes in business. All day, every day, in American business and internationally, people walk away from en-counters with their employees or their superiors frustrated because neither one of the people was clear about who was going to do what, for whom, by when, using what resources. Painting a clear picture of the target will solve this problem.

If our charge is to satisfy employees by doing what they request—"Paint me a clear picture of the target"—how do we do that?

The first way is by remembering a fundamental maxim that is often overlooked. It makes eminent sense when you examine it.

Everyone Wasn't Raised at Your House

More performance management discussions have gone awry from not remembering this maxim than from any other in this book. We tend to fail in interactions because we assume that the people with whom we are talking have had the same experiences we've had, been trained by the same people, been formed by the same family, and know the same things.

It's patently obvious that this is not so. We need to remember this as we give direction, backing and filling around holes in our employee's knowledge. Never assume that, just because we know it or would do it, they would know the same things and behave in the same ways.

An example from the quick-service restaurant industry might be useful.

As one fast-food company hired new employees, the new employee would be put to work at the simpler tasks of the business—sweeping the parking lot, emptying trash, clearing the dining tables, or cleaning the dining room or the restrooms. Let's look in on a scenario where an assistant manager is asking new employee Eager Beaver to clean the dining room.

ASSISTANT MANAGER: Well, Eager, you've finished all your paperwork and we've got your uniforms. Are you ready to go to work?

EAGER BEAVER: Yes, sir!

ASSISTANT MANAGER: Okay! I'd like you to clean the dining room.

EAGER BEAVER: Okey dokey.

ASSISTANT MANAGER: Let's take a look at it. *Surveys a room with overflowing waste cans, trash on the floor, messy tables, windows with fingerprints, and rubbish everywhere.* I want you to clean it up like it was the dining room at your house.

EAGER BEAVER: Okay, coach. Say—it's already cleaner than my dining room. Whatcha want me to do next?

Clearly, Eager wasn't raised at his manager's house. That's not Eager's fault, but it is the manager's responsibility to *mitigate against this situation with clear, precise expectation-setting*.

Here's a corollary to the maxim, "Everybody wasn't raised at your house." Throughout the world, you will hear managers say, "But that's just *common sense!!*" But it's *not* common sense, or at least not yet. First, we have to paint a clear picture of the target. Until then, your expectations are neither *common* nor *sensical*.

Common Sense Ain't Near as Common as It Used to Be

When I'm working with groups and talking about common sense, I ask this question: "How many of you know which side of a horse you should mount from?" Generally, less than half the class knows the correct answer.

A hundred years ago, knowing how to mount a horse was just common sense—unless you really *liked* to walk. Now we've got cars and trains and airplanes and subways, and people don't ride horses any more. The side of a horse from which to mount is no longer common sense. For years, it was common sense. Now it's not. And that's the risk of "common sense." (By the way, you mount a horse from the left side.)

Because the notion of "common sense" changes, and because not everyone has had the same formative experiences, we have to make sure we all are working with the same definitions.

Several years ago, a friend of mine (a bright, articulate man with an earned PhD) came to me and asked me to develop a marketing plan for him.

I know what a marketing plan is; the first decade of my working life was spent in the marketing side of business. So I wrote him a first-rate marketing plan, one worth far more than what he paid me to develop it. The plan included several key objectives and the strategies and tactics needed to achieve those objectives. I even drilled down to the execution level with timelines and action plans. It was an airtight marketing plan—and one of my best pieces of work.

When I handed it to him, he was woefully disappointed. He hadn't wanted a marketing *plan*; he wanted a marketing *executive*. He hadn't wanted me to *develop* it; he had wanted me to *execute* it.

Who was wrong here? Nobody. And everybody. He asked me for *what he thought he wanted*, and I gave him *what I thought he asked for*. Both of us *assumed* a common language and a common understanding. From that assumption we disappointed each other gravely, and eventually ruptured the relationship. And that is the great risk of unclear expectations—as we disappoint each other (with unclear expectations and the attendant re-work and frustration), we create fissures in working relationships that can become outright crevasses.

Painting a clear picture of the target is a fundamental obligation of all managers as they think about their contract with the people they manage. *People can't give you what you want unless they know what that is.* And because they are not clairvoyant, you have to tell them. Or—better yet—sometimes you have to *show* them.

My grandfather was a Gulf Oil distributor in the Triangle area of North Carolina. In the mid-twentieth century, I rode around with him as he went from service station to service station talking to dealers about how to attract more business.

(This was on the front end of the curve as Americans began to travel widely on summer vacations.)

My grandfather's theory, which was borne out in practice, was this: clean restrooms attract the wives, and the wives tell the husbands where to stop. A big issue for him was that all his service stations have immaculate restrooms.

My grandfather was a solidly built man in his late fifties, and he would inspect the bathrooms at every station where we stopped. If he found the bathrooms clean, he would thank the manager, tell him why clean restrooms were important, and move on.

If the restrooms weren't clean, my grandfather didn't have a tantrum. He figured it was his job to show the station operator what he meant by clean. It was his job to "paint a clear picture of the target." Rather than *having a fit*, he *had a demonstration*.

He would take off his straw hat and hang it on the doorknob. He would take off his suit coat and hang it on the door. Then he would roll up his sleeves, tuck his tie in his shirt pocket, get the cleaning supplies out of the trunk of his car, and clean the bathroom, on his hands and knees, in his suit pants.

When he was finished, he would look at the service station manager—who was generally aghast—and say to him, "Now, do you see what I mean by a clean bathroom?"

"Yes sir, yes sir, I see what you mean."

"This is how I want it to look every time I come back

from now on. Do you understand why this is important? Do you have any questions?"

Generally the person knew why it was important, and had no questions. And generally, when my grandfather came back the next time, the bathrooms were clean.

Why did my grandfather get such good results? One, he believed in encouraging people, so his habit was to offer them carrots, not sticks. Two, he painted for them a clear picture of the target. And three, my grandfather didn't assume that they knew what he meant by "clean." "Clean" is different things to different people. To get the kind of clean *you* want, paint a clear picture of *your* target.

To Be Worth a Damn, a Goal Must Be SMART

The way you paint a clear picture of the target is by using SMART goals. SMART is an acronym, and you'll see it presented in Figure 3-1.

Here's what it stands for:

❦ S IS FOR *SPECIFIC*. You must know *exactly* what you want. Do you want *lunch*, or do you want a *Big Burgher, hold the sauce, double onions, no ketchup*?

SMART GOALS

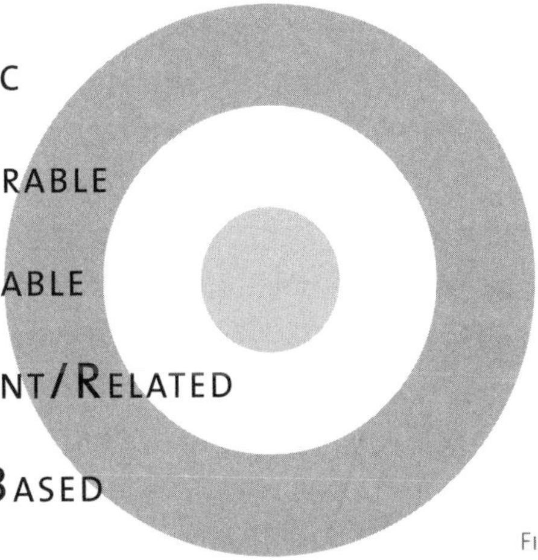

SPECIFIC

MEASURABLE

ATTAINABLE

RELEVANT/**R**ELATED

TIME-**B**ASED

FIGURE 3-1

   ❧ M IS FOR *MEASURABLE*. You need to talk to the employee about how you're going to measure performance—what the measurements methods are, how you are going to collect the data, who's going to collect the data, and when the data will be collected.

   ❧ A IS FOR *ATTAINABLE*. The goal needs to be difficult enough to make the employee work but not so impossible that she will never reach it.

   ❧ R IS FOR *RELATED*. Relate the goal to a personal goal of the employee, to a work group goal, and to an overarching corporate goal—a goal that the employee's efforts will help the company attain.

🐎 T IS FOR *TIME-BASED*. That is, set a time when the project is due, along with an intermediate date so you can see how the project is moving along.

Most Work Gets Done the Day Before It's Due

My fundamental belief is that most work in life gets done the day before it is due. There is no need to argue about this or get mad about it or wish that people would change. What you do is use this knowledge by setting intermediate dates and following up on those dates to see what progress has been made toward final completion of the project. This method works equally well whether you are managing your own performance or that of someone else.

A DETAILED EXAMINATION OF THE SMART METHOD OF GOAL SETTING

Let's look at the SMART method point by point..

☞ SMART: Specific

The *S* in SMART stands for *Specific*. We've already partially illustrated *Specific* with the Big Burgher example, but let's amplify what we've learned. In the Burgher example, we were *specific* about the condiments we wanted. Other places that cry out for specificity include: What resources will be available? What's the budget? Do you have a sample I can go by? Are any other people available to help me do this project? What's the priority? How will this influence my other projects?

This part of our SMART acronym is where we deal with *specification* of the project. (Not surprisingly, *specification* and *specific* are both derived from the same root word as the word *spectacle*. They all communicate something about being able to *see clearly*.) After we've dealt with the specifics of the task, we must address how we will measure progress.

☞ SMART: Measurable

The *M* in SMART stands for *Measurable*. I once had an employee who was chronically late. In exasperation, I told this employee, "If you're *ever* late again, I'm going to fire you." The employee looked at me, deadpan, and said, "Your watch or mine?"

That's precisely the point I'm trying to make: you have to decide *before* the conversation *who's keeping score* and *how the score will be kept*, in order to prevent yourself from getting into unfortunate situations.

Figure out what the measurement methods are, and make sure that you're measuring the things that matter.

What You Count Is What You're Going to Get

I confessed earlier that I once got a job as a national sales manager for an automotive battery company, and the job was bigger than my skills to do it. Now you get to benefit from one of my mistakes.

When I took that job, I realized that most of the people were not working very hard. So I set for them a clear performance management standard. I asked each salesperson to make more calls, intuitively assuming that if people made calls, they would make sales.

Wrong. Wrong. Wrong. People made lots of calls; I had call reports that weighed so much my desk was beginning to sag. But nothing was happening. No business was being generated. Why? I *was counting the wrong thing*. I asked for calls, so people made *calls*. They just weren't making *sales*. ("Why bother? That's not what he's counting!")

Therefore, being the bright, articulate, incisive leader that I was, I changed the target. Salespeople were now evaluated on new accounts, because I figured that if we opened new accounts, customers would buy more products. So I recalibrated the target: *we're not just looking for calls, we're looking for new accounts!*

Wrong again. We had accounts set up at swimming pools. We had accounts set up at hairdressers. We had accounts offering automotive batteries in adult bookstores and at massage parlors. But nobody was doing repeat business. Batteries were just sitting in those outlets going stale. Why? Because people were selling, but they were selling the wrong prospects. Not their fault—my fault. *I was counting the wrong thing.*

On the third iteration, I got it right. We began to count new, profitable business from new customers, and that led us to the performance we sought. But it took me three tries to get it right, and those two wrong turns cost us time and money. I frustrated my employees and I frustrated myself because I was not getting the performance I sought. And *I was not getting the performance I sought* because *I was counting the wrong things.* It was only when I began to count new, profitable business from new customers that I got the results I sought. (And even then, I was not measuring anything that encouraged good service to existing accounts. But that's another story!)

So, think through the targets you set. Remember that it's okay to ask 'em to work. But when you ask 'em to work, you have to paint them a clear picture of the target. And—as you paint that clear picture—make sure that what you count is what you want. Because *what you count is what you're going to get.*

☞ SMART: Attainable

The *A* in SMART is the one that folks often don't think about, and it's vital. As I often tell the managers in my training classes, "People who don't think they can succeed won't try."

I'll illustrate with a story. During a break in a training workshop, we all get in the elevator and go to the top story of a twenty-five-story building. We step out onto the roof and walk to the edge. I inform you that I've had a lot of luck teaching people how to fly. I say, "I'm going to give you about fifteen minutes of ground school, then one at a time, I'm going to let you glide off the building and see how it works. Who'd be interested in going first?"

Invariably, no one speaks up. Why? They don't think it's *attainable*. (Although often some wag says, "You know, I work best by *demonstration*. You jump off first and show me how it works, and I'll go next.") The goal has got to be attainable, or employees won't try.

Conversely, we all remember the childhood tale of the tortoise and the hare. In this case, the hare's task (a footrace with a stupid turtle) was just too *easy*. He lay down on the job for a quick snooze and the turtle waxed him.

When, as managers, we set goals for our folks, we are looking for that delicate middle ground, the sweet spot. The goals have to be tough enough to be challenging, but not so hard as to be disheartening. It's a tough—and important—challenge.

☞ SMART: Relevant/Related

The *R* in SMART stands for *Relevant*, or *Related*. This speaks to our obligation to tie the objective back to a carrot the employee wants to embrace or a stick the employee wants to avoid. As we work our way through relating the target to the employee's carrots and sticks, we are most effective when our target is relevant on many levels; that is, when the goal has a personal reward/consequence for the employee, and also a larger (either work group or corporate) reward/consequence. Goals work best when—by helping the company or work group reach a goal—the employee also reaches a personal goal. You may remember this as *goal alignment* from Chapter 2.

☞ SMART: Time-Based

Finally, the *T* in SMART stands for *Time-Based*. Time speaks to the notion that most people do things only when their performance is being measured by a time goal. If you owed the IRS money and taxes weren't due by April 15, would you have filed your taxes yet? No chance. But you know that if you don't file them, you're in deep trouble. It's not that you *like* filing them, it's that *they're keeping score*. The time deadline is midnight on April 15, so you get them there at 11:59 and consider yourself having been there well ahead of time.

SMART. It's not exactly brain surgery. It certainly isn't inordinately complex. But it will revolutionize how you manage, and it will eliminate 80 percent of your "Aw, crap," managerial experiences. Because your team will know—up front and in the open—what you need, how you're gonna measure it, why it matters, and when it's due.

Set SMART goals. Paint a clear picture of your target.

⇒ MAXIMS ON EXPECTATIONS ⇐

Paint a clear picture of the target.

I can't hit a target I can't see.

Everyone wasn't raised at your house.

Common sense ain't near as common as it used to be.

To be worth a damn, a goal must be SMART.

Most work gets done the day before it's due.

What you count is what you're going to get.

QUESTIONS FOR REFLECTION

1. When is a time that your manager failed to paint you a clear picture of the target? What happened? Who was more frustrated—you or your manager?

2. Everyone wasn't raised at your house. What are some of the things you learned at your house that you've been surprised that *all* people don't know?

3. Have you ever counted the wrong thing in setting performance standards? What happened?

4. Reflect on the SMART model. What point do you find yourself consistently falling short on?

CHALLENGE FOR APPLICATION

How can you more clearly paint pictures of the targets you expect your employees to hit? What do you think will happen if you do this? When—exactly—are you going to start?

4

COACHING: THEM THAT CAN, DOES—THEM THAT TEACHES ARE PRICELESS

If painting a clear picture of the target is the starting point for pulling maximum performance out of those we manage and oversee, teaching and coaching are the next steps.

Our society has a funny perception of teachers, and of coaches, too, for that matter. Coaches—at least coaches who win often and well—are held in high esteem by our society, lionized for their tactical minds, and compensated at astronomical levels for the success they pull out of their followers. Teachers, on the other hand, are often forced to do their work with limited resources in aging buildings while working with learners who would rather be somewhere else. The juxtaposition is particularly poignant because *these people are in the same profession*. Teachers and coaches are both in the business of transferring knowledge from one head to another, the business of helping learners become the very best they can be at the task before them. This is also the challenge before managers called upon to coach and teach in business and corporate environments.

Our conflicting understanding of (and appreciation for) teachers is reflected in what we say about them and their work. You may have heard the old saying, "Those who can, do. Those who can't, teach." This is as much nonsense as the old phrase, "If you're so smart, why aren't you rich?" Smartness and richness are only mildly correlated, if at all. And of the various kinds of intelligence sprinkled across the human spectrum, the intelligence for making large amounts of money is neither the rarest nor the most valuable.

Conversely, the capacity to engender in others a love of learning is a scarce and valuable talent. The ability to transfer from one person to another the skills needed to do a task, and the motivation to do it well, is "work." It *is* "doing something." So teaching and coaching are critical skills. If you have a native talent for this work, you should thank whatever Power it is you thank for all good gifts. And, if you don't have a native talent, hard work and discipline can make a dramatic difference in your ability to teach.

If you wish to develop teaching and coaching skills, you will soon realize that there is much to the seeming ease with which teachers and coaches impart information and draw superior performance from their teams. Fortunately, there are some maxims that can help inform our understanding of good teaching and coaching. These guidelines can help us to move from whatever level we now occupy to a level of increased competence and facility as business teachers and coaches.

Common Sense Ain't Near as Common as It Used to Be II

As we begin reflecting on how we can teach and coach more effectively, it is helpful to examine the operative assumptions that inform our work. For our first coaching maxim, we'll revisit an old friend from Chapter 3: "Common sense ain't near as common as it used to be!"

Though not the most finely crafted grammatical statement you will ever read, our initial maxim captures a fundamental truth. You may have, at some time in your business career, been exposed to the old saying, "Whenever you assume, you make an 'ass' out of 'u' and 'me.'"

Our common sense maxim amplifies this notion. As teachers, we often forget the baseline level at which *we began* acquiring information on a topic. We assume a level of understanding that is neither fair to our learners nor helpful to our teaching challenge. Remembering that everyone wasn't raised at our house, we acknowledge that what is common sense to us may be completely unknown to the learner with whom we're interacting.

To counteract this, we begin with the basics: definitions of key terms, explanations of fundamental processes, articulation of the reasons behind what we are doing, and the ultimate business objective we seek as an outcome. Once we have done this, we are ready to reflect on differences in learning styles we may encounter among our learners.

People Learn in Different Ways. To Be Effective, Teach in the Learner's Most-Preferred Style

People learn in different ways. To be an effective teacher, you must teach in the way most preferred by the learner. Some people are *oral learners*; they learn only as they speak. Many of these gravitate toward teaching so that they can fully master their topics. Others are *kinesthetic experiential learners*; they must learn by touching, by engaging manually the item with which they are learning. For these kinds of learners, no amount of reading will engender learning as fast as a very brief period of touching.

A third group of people are *aural learners*; they learn well by hearing. They can learn more in a fifteen-minute lecture than they can in three hours of painstakingly plodding through a book of instructions or directions. Finally, there are *visual learners*. They learn by reading. These people are the instruction manuals' major friends, and can master a topic thoroughly with two or three hours of careful review of a tightly written instruction packet or a well-produced

LEARNER TABLE TYPES

LEARN TYPE	CHARACTERIZED BY	POSSIBLE OCCUPATIONS
Oral Learners	Learn by saying. Have to "talk to know."	Teachers, professors, salespeople, marketing professionals, singers, copywriters, consultants
Kinesthetic/ Experiential Learners	Learn by touching and doing. Need to physically engage the object.	Engineers, architects, sculptors, dancers, chefs, mechanics, technicians, surgeons, performance artists, athletes
Aural Learners	Learn by listening. Can hear something and remember it.	Musicians, psychologists, psychiatrists, consultants
Visual Learners	Learn by seeing or reading. For readers, often described as having a photographic memory.	Accountants, attorneys, graphic artists, painters, designers

FIGURE 4-1

training video. Unfortunately, there are far fewer of these than most teaching curricula assume. To be fully effective, we must use *all* the teaching methods so that our entire population of learners is fully able to master the body of information we are trying to communicate. The table in Figure 4-1 presents a fleshed-out view of learning styles.

A couple of examples here might prove useful. One of my associates in our consulting business has worked with us for a number of years as a facilitator for video skill sessions. She is a tremendously bright, highly competent person—a joy to work with in every way.

In my working with her, however, I made several erroneous assumptions about her learning style. My assumptions made it difficult for her to learn the skills she needed in our work together. I assumed (remember our earlier caution against assumptions!) that my friend would learn in the same ways I like to learn. So I tried to teach her how to operate a relatively complicated piece of equipment by *talking* to her about it and demonstrating as I went. I was telling her (aural) and showing her (visual) how to use the equipment. It did not work.

After some period of frustration, she looked at me and said, "This is not how I like to learn. Your talking is confusing me and your demonstrations are distracting me. Be quiet. Leave me alone. Give me the instruction manual and let me figure it out for myself." I did. She did. And all's well that ends well.

I was fortunate in this instance because I was working with someone who *knew* her preferred learning style. My colleague was able to ask for the teaching and learning methods that worked best for her. And I, eventually, was able to respond in a way that was helpful to her. You may not always be as fortunate as I was; your learners may not be able to *tell* you how they like to learn. Fortunately, there's another way to determine learning styles.

If You Observe and Listen Long Enough, People Will Tell You How They Like to Learn

We reviewed an observation similar to this in the chapter on motivation. Now we will examine how people telegraph to us their most-preferred learning styles. And the best way to illustrate this is to roll the tape on a familiar scenario.

A cozy little couple has bought a new gas grill. Flush with the pride of ownership, they bring it home and begin to assemble it in their basement playroom. The wife (an accountant) carefully removes all the pieces and sorts them into appropriate piles to check against the parts list. Meanwhile, her husband (a salesman) goes to change clothes.

When he returns, she has inventoried all the parts and is halfway through the instructions. Ignoring all her hard work, he plops down in the center of the room, picks up the largest part, and asks, "Where do you reckon this goes?"

We need play this out no further. We've seen it a thousand times in life and on television sitcoms, and many of us have lived it as well. The wife here is—both by training and inclination—a visual learner. She has sorted and counted and now she is reading—all playing off her native strengths as a visual learner. The husband, in contrast, seems to be a mix of kinesthetic and oral. He jumps into the middle of the pile, grabs the largest part, and starts talking.

Neither of them is right; neither is wrong. They are just *very* different. And—by how they interact with this project—each is telegraphing to the other how they best like to learn.

Your learners are doing the same thing—telegraphing to you how they like to learn by their everyday actions and reactions to events around them.

A final example, this one from my own life experience. My wife is a gifted participant in all manner of water sports and spent much of her childhood on and around the water. I, on the other hand, was a land-locked country boy when we married. And—while I could swim—I knew nothing of sailing, skiing, fishing, windsurfing, or any other of the myriad activities she finds so delightful. Some years after our marriage, she began to try to teach me how to sail a sailboat. It was not a Kodak moment.

Laura is an excellent teacher, and she carefully began to teach me how to sail with the methods that worked best for her. She gave me clear and precise (to my way of thinking, constraining and overly controlling) instructions about how to tack, how to come about, why we should avoid jibing, and on and on, *ad infinitum, ad nauseam, ad divorcium.*

Unlike my friend in the previous example, I did not know about preferred learning styles and was unable to coach Laura in how best to teach me. Rather, I fell back on the time-honored relational model of screaming at her whenever she told me to do something I didn't like. Needless to say, screaming did not calm the troubled waters of our maritime relationship. I soon realized that if I didn't find another way to learn, I was going to be sailing into the sunset alone. This was not an outcome I sought.

So, I began to rise early in the morning on the summer days when we were down on the water, and I taught myself to sail with two-hour sails between six and eight o'clock in the morning. It was this experience that made me realize that I am an experiential learner. I learn only by doing, by touching, by feeling, by experiencing; any other form of teaching, while it may provide me with some facts, will never help me engage the information as fully as touching, tasting, feeling, and doing.

Discovered Learning Always Beats Revealed Learning

Whatever the teaching style preferred by our learner, and whatever way we teach best, the outcome we seek is always the same: *discovered learning*. That is, we seek the moment when our learner has an "Aha!" experience and discovers the immediate relevance of—or a full understanding about—

the topic we are examining. And discovered learning always beats revealed learning. It is discovered learning that moves knowledge to the hard drive of our brains, hits the "save" button, and enables us years later to remember what it was we learned, and why.

Consider this simple example of discovered learning: a small girl is playing near a hot item in the kitchen. Her mother points dramatically to the pot or plate and says, "Hot. Do not touch. No. Hot." In that teaching, the mother has carefully tried to teach her daughter through *revealed* learning. She has *revealed* to the child that the item is hot and will burn her. Having carefully listened to her mother, the child will then toddle over to the item, touch it herself, and burst into a heartrending wail. The child has now had an experience of *discovered* learning. She is now much more likely to remember the "hot"-ness of the item, and the reasons for not touching it should the circumstance occur again.

Repeated often enough, this experience will do several things: one, it will change the way the mother teaches the child, realizing that the child will learn from her own discovered experience; two, it will teach the child to trust the mother, realizing that when the mother says something is harmful, hurtful, or hot, she is telling the truth; and three, slowly, event by event, the child will learn what to do and what not to do.

Discovered knowledge always beats revealed knowledge. Our job, as coaches and teachers in the business world, is to provide safe places where learners can have discovered knowledge without killing themselves, bankrupting the business, or having other ruinous effects on the commerce in which we are involved.

Let's examine a couple of ways that, in the world of business and government, teachers and coaches have sought to help learners gain discovered learning experiences. One example that comes immediately to mind is the use of simulators in the training of nuclear power plant operators and airline pilots. In both these examples, the learners can be presented with dire circumstances that require immediate, decisive, correct action to prevent catastrophic loss of life. The learners can test themselves against these circumstances, responding as if the threat of catastrophe were real, while still knowing that they can survive to learn another day. This is what makes this methodology so powerful. It's also a reason the case method has been adopted in so many American business schools—cases being a simulated form of management interaction. All of these examples allow students to *discover* their learning in a way that promotes lifelong retention of the lessons learned.

Different from—but allied to—our maxim that discovered learning beats revealed learning are the next two maxims.

People Never Argue with Their Own Data

Bob Pike is one of America's foremost trainers of trainers, and I am in his debt for this maxim.[1] This is related to *discovered learning* because when folks have an experience of *discovered learning*, they are developing their own data. These data will help them load the learning to the hard drive of their brain and be able to recall it on demand.

As teachers and coaches, we help people develop their own data by facilitating and listening, *not* telling. This can be frustrating, because—in the short term—it is more time-consuming than telling. In the longer term, however, it is far more efficient. It's more efficient because, as people talk in a facilitated learning environment, the discussion feeds multiple learning styles. The oral learners get to talk and the aural learners get to hear. Even the kinesthetic learners get to play with ideas, turning them over figuratively and touching them with the fingers of their imaginations. And in developing these ideas—these data, if you will—our learners more fully explore the topic and are more likely to store it in their long-term memory.

It Is Easier to Listen People into Learning Than to Talk Them into Learning

In many ways, teaching is a motivational situation. Sure, it's a *specific* kind of motivational situation, but it's motivation all the same.

And a primary way to motivate people to learn is to listen to them: what their problems are, what matters to them, what specific things they need to know to grow. Then we can package our teaching in a way that meets learners' needs and builds off what we have heard them say.

All of these ideas we have visited are well and good. Still, they cry out for a disciplined process to walk us through the task of teaching and coaching in a business context. That is why I developed the COACH model: to help myself remember the key components of the coaching interaction. The model also ensures that I give learners the information they need to do a task well, on target, to specs, when required.

To Be a Good Coach, Use the COACH Model

Let's walk through this model item by item. We find the COACH model in Figure 4-2. Each of the five letters in the COACH model stands for one key concept related to teaching people how to do things.

☞ COACH: Content

The first *C* in COACH stands for *Content*. Content includes the "what" of our teaching: what is it they need to know, what is it they need to learn, what are the steps in the process? And beyond the "what," content also includes the "why."

Adult learners like to know "why" as well as "what." One of our tasks is to lay before them the reasons that they

CONTENT

ORGANIZATION

APPROACH

CANDIDATE

HEADLINES

FIGURE 4-2

are being taught a particular subject. Is it to be more efficient? Is it to be safer? Is it to better serve the customer or company?

As children we often heard, "Because I told you to," as the answer to "Why?" And some managers try it even now. It doesn't work. Adults want to know the professional underpinnings for any action that their managers request. We also need to communicate to employees "what's in it for me" as we lay out the content of a teaching. Beyond any professional "why," there must also be a personal "why." A "why" that answers the query posed by WII-FM. (Don't forget that WII-FM is the most powerful radio station in the world.)

☞ COACH: Organization

After we have reflected on our content points, listing them as they pop into our minds and fully exhausting everything that needs to be presented, we move to O in our COACH model. We reflect on how to *organize* our points. In which *sequence* should these items be taught?

The issue of organization does not often occur to people, particularly coaches in the business world, and that's a pity because *the order* in which something is taught can have a tremendous bearing on how long it is retained. Our tendency is to fall into the trap of teaching everything we teach in sequential order. And sequential order is an excellent way for teaching some processes; I use it often myself. But we should *choose* the order in which we teach things, not fall into sequential order by default.

There are myriad other ways in which we could order our material. For people who are completely new to a process, we might teach them the *easiest things* first. This will help them build confidence in their skills and their ability to do something productive. In cases where we're teaching information that has a high critical-safety index, we might *begin with the safety issues*, reasoning that a learner who's not committed to safety should never learn the rest of the process.

We can also *teach in order of frequency,* a teaching style often used in helping people become familiar with troubleshooting pieces of complicated mechanical equipment. If 80 percent of the breakdowns are caused by 3 percent of the malfunctions, clearly the best thing to learn first is the 3 percent that will solve 80 percent of the problems. So that would drive the order in which we taught the material.

As we think about organization in our coaching model, the key work for us is to *be aware that we have choices.* We do not *have to* teach in sequence. We *can* teach in sequence, or we can teach in priority. We can begin with safety first, or we can begin with frequent occurrences. We can teach the easiest things first, or we can organize in some other way.

Our choice of how to organize our material needs to be just that, a *choice*—not a willy-nilly, haphazard, falling-into that is governed by nothing but chance.

☞ COACH: Approach

When we have moved beyond the ranking of our content and the organizing of it into the order that makes the most sense, we then begin to think about our *approach* to communicating the material. How is it we will teach this? This is where an early aphorism from this chapter, *"People learn in different ways, teach in the way preferred by the learner,"* comes into play. We marry our understanding of the material to the person to whom we will be presenting it, and choose a way that will best fit both the material and the learner.

Some things can best be learned by reading; others can only be learned by seeing.

And as we learned earlier, there are people who can learn only by saying, or hearing, or touching. Our challenge in selecting a teaching approach is to identify the approach that best marries the needs of the learner with the demands of the material.

Often the best approach to teaching is one that teaches in multiple ways. Merwyn Hayes is the godfather of training in my region of the country; he introduced me to the Tell-Show-Do-Feedback model presented in Figure 4-3.

The *Telling* part of this model can take several forms: reading, discussion, or lecture. Some combination of these will meet the learning needs of visual, oral, and aural learners.

Showing builds on the foundation laid in telling, and speaks to the needs of visual learners again.

TELL

SHOW

DO

FEEDBACK

FIGURE 4-3

Doing is where kinesthetic learners get their needs meet. When accompanied by narrative, this is also a good way for aural and oral learners to acquire knowledge.

The fourth portion—*Feedback*—can meet the needs of various learners. Videotaped playback allows folks to see themselves (discovered learning) and understand where they need to improve. Discussion helps both oral and aural learners draw important learning from feedback. The key in selecting our approach is to choose the approach that best suits our material and our learner—the candidate to whom we'll be addressing our message.

☞ COACH: Candidate

Having reflected on the content, the organization of that content, and the teaching approach, we then move to the second *C* in our COACH model, where we reflect on the *Candidate*. Who is this person before us? Who is this person who will be learning the materials? What is his experience level with this or similar work? What is his aptitude for this work? What is his motivation for learning the work? How does he best like to learn? All of these things come into play as we shape our teaching and coaching plan.

A good way to consider all these issues is to ask the candidate questions. Give the candidate input into shaping her training plan, while retaining your ownership of the overall process. A candidate is much more likely to "own" a positive outcome from the training if she helped to develop the plan, and she is much more likely to remember the training if you can make it memorable with good headlines.

☞ COACH: Headlines

Finally, the *H* in our coaching model begs us to reduce all of our teaching (or at least the core concepts) to an easy-to-remember *headline*. Headlines will help our learner remember what we've said and—beyond what we've said—*remember why it matters*.

Headlines come in a variety of forms. Our COACH acronym is an example of a headline, as was the SMART acronym we used in Chapter 3, when we reflected on how to paint clear pictures of our targets.

But all headlines are not acronyms. A headline can be a number of words related to a topic that all begin with the same letter, for instance "The Six Ds of Delegation." A headline could incorporate rhyme (I once worked with a landscaping firm that described their competitors as folks who "mow, blow, and go" in juxtaposition to their own, professional landscaping skills.) Beyond rhyming, acronyms, and alliteration, headlines can incorporate in-vogue advertising slogans ("Just do it" being a shopworn example of this).

The task at hand is not to be *cute* but to be *memorable*. Headlines are only as good as the ease with which they help our learners remember what was said, why it matters, and how to recall it in appropriate situations in their work life.

So, there are five steps in our COACH model. Good coaching requires an intense scrutiny of the *content* we will be teaching, a clear rhyme or reason to our *organization* of that content, and a disciplined understanding of which *approach* we will use in teaching our content. We must then carefully reflect on the *candidate* whom we will be teaching, and develop *headlines* that will help the candidate load the material onto the hard drive of his brain.

At this point, it should be clear that teaching of others *is* work. Managers often think that *after* they teach somebody something, *then* the two of them can begin working. But the moment the teaching begins, the work begins. It is a hard, demanding discipline for which only a few people have a natural facility. It can, however, be learned, and the COACH model is an excellent way to discipline yourself before you begin to interact with a learner.

In the end, while difficult, coaching is not complicated. In fact, Bear Bryant (who was unquestionably a successful coach whether or not you are a fan of the Crimson Tide) reduced all of coaching to five steps—five things winning teams want. I first saw this listing from my friend and colleague Jerry Hancock;[2] it is presented below.

Five things winning teams need to know:

1. Tell me what you expect from me. (As we've said here, paint a clear picture of the target.)

2. Give me an opportunity to perform. (As we've learned, this is where you COACH.)

3. Let me know how I'm getting along. (We'll review this in Chapter 5.)

4. Give me guidance when I need it. (This is also in Chapter 5.)

5. Reward me according to my contribution. (We'll cover this topic further in Chapter 6.)

Coaching is hard work. Don't deceive yourself into thinking you can walk into a coaching interaction and "make it up." It will not work. On the other hand, the benefits of successful coaching interactions far outweigh the investment in time required to be successful.

Learn to coach, and you're well on your way to a winning team.

⇒ MAXIMS ON COACHING ⇒

Common sense ain't near as common as it used to be.

People learn in different ways. To be effective, teach in the learner's most-preferred style.

If you observe and listen long enough, people will tell you how they like to learn.

Discovered learning always beats revealed learning.

People never argue with their own data.

It is easier to listen people into learning than to talk them into learning.

To be a good coach, use the COACH model.

Adult learners like to know why.

QUESTIONS FOR REFLECTION

1. What is your most-preferred learning style? Are you a visual learner? Kinesthetic? Oral? Aural? How has your most-preferred style influenced how you teach?

2. What examples of "discovered learning" can you recall from your own life? Why did they stick as they did?

3. Why do you think people never argue with their own data?

4. Can you think of a time in your life when you were told "what" but not "why"? What impact did this have on your ability to learn?

CHALLENGE FOR APPLICATION

Think about a recent situation where you have had to teach someone. Which of the COACH steps did you remember to follow? What did you leave out? How might you handle the situation differently given what you know now?

5

FEEDBACK AND PERFORMANCE MANAGEMENT: WHAT YOU REWARD IS WHAT YOU GET

People Will *Re*spect What You *Ex*pect If You *In*spect

I remember the event as clearly as if it happened only yesterday. A client of mine was holding a training workshop. The focus of the afternoon session on the second day was how to pull superior performance out of employees. A grizzled veteran of the management wars stood up and made an impassioned pronouncement that ended with, "People will *re*spect what you *ex*pect if you *in*spect!"

Following this declaration, he plopped back down in his chair and waited for some response from his teammates. He didn't have to wait long, because their nods of assent and vocal affirmation indicated that he had hit upon a key, essential truth in the managerial world. People *will* respect what we expect if we inspect. And it is the process of inspecting that *generates* the respect. Reflect again on our example of speed limits. There you are, speeding merrily along, when traffic suddenly slows and you see a forest of brake lights ahead. Did the entire motoring universe have an attack of conscience and repent of speeding? Hardly! They had an attack of *fear*, because a highway patrol car was seen just up the road, and the officer was inspecting that 65-mile-per-hour expectation! Now *that* gets respect!

Performance management is grounded upon painting a clear picture of the target/expectation at the beginning of the process. We cannot measure performance against standards that have not been articulated, codified, and communicated to the workers. That, in fact, is why governments spend tens of thousands of dollars every year posting speed limit signs alongside major highways. Communicating standards, however, is not enough—as any traveler on our nation's highways has seen. It is in the *measurement* of performance that we often find managers failing their followers, their companies, and themselves.

How many times in your organization have you labored long and hard over a project only to have it become a nice, pristine, unused binder on your boss's bookshelf? You got no feedback on the quality of your work—what you did well or how you could improve it. If this has happened to you, then your company is an organization that may paint clear pictures of the targets but fails to measure performance against those targets.

Now reflect on what happens to your motivation level when you slave over a project, do your absolute best to achieve perfection, and get no feedback at all. Your motivation slumps—you didn't get any carrots. And in addition to getting no carrots, you also got no specific, targeted feedback identifying how you fell short, and how to improve next time. You begin—as we all do—to lose *re*spect for management expectations that go un*in*spected. Or—as we learned in the unit on goal setting—what management counts is what management gets, so count the right stuff.

What You Count Is What You Get, So Count the Right Things

I once knew an old-school manager who evaluated his sales people in several peculiar ways. This manager had grown up in a time when automobiles were a novelty, and travel by car was rare and difficult. His business was automotive-related, and he was fascinated by the car. Still, it was a surprise to me when I realized that he evaluated his salespeople's productivity by *the number of miles a salesperson drove in a day*! His theory: the more miles you drive, the harder you are working.

Because this manager was famous for follow-up, his people ran up miles like long-haul truck drivers. What he counted was what he got!

A second peculiar performance measure—again by the same manager—was a salesperson's rate of business-card usage. He would constantly hold up for acclamation the salespeople who quickly went through a box of five hundred business cards. His theory: the more business cards you use, the more sales calls you have made.

Once again, what he counted was what he got. Employees respected his expectation because he was famous for inspecting. Years passed before I realized that two-thirds of the sales department threw away eight-tenths of their business cards every quarter.

Don't Confuse Motion with Progress

What we measure is what gets done. We need to measure the right stuff. Measuring business card usage rather than profitable account generation will yield you lots of invoices from your business card printer, but few new accounts. Measuring miles driven per day will yield you odometers in the thousands, while your sales numbers are big fat goose eggs.

My old-school manager friend was confusing motion with progress. He *assumed*—as I did in my early life as a sales manager—that business card usage was linked to sales increases. That more miles intuitively equaled more calls and new accounts. He counted activities, not outcomes. So he got activity *as* an outcome.

The tragedy here is that measuring the activities—with no correction for specific outcomes—can actually take an organization backward. Think about it: measuring business card usage (with no concomitant measurement of increased profitable sales) just drives up sales expense and drives down profits. Likewise, rewarding miles driven yields shopworn, exhausted cars, increased fleet maintenance expense, and a rapidly depreciating stable of automobiles, with no offsetting increase in sales. What you count is what you'll get. So don't confuse motion with progress—or activities with outcomes.

It's hard to admit it to ourselves, but even highly motivated types like you and me are watching to see what management counts. In the early 1980s, I worked for Sara Lee Corporation in the L'eggs Pantyhose Division. During that experience I learned a great deal about management—both from my superiors and from my peers. Following one round of managerial musical chairs, I was placed under a new manager and began to try to learn how to work well with this person. I was immediately struck by how often this manager would request information from me about ancillary topics not directly related to any specific project. The more of these requests I got, the more frantic I became. I quickly realized that there would be no time left to do my profit-generating work if I chased all the rabbits he flushed out and dumped into my inbox. Finally, in utter frustration and despair, I went to a peer of mine who had recently finished a stint working with this manager.

"What in the world can I do with all these requests? I'm drowning in penciled notes asking me to check up on one thing or track down another. I can't get my work done."

My colleague looked at me knowingly and responded, "I know. I faced the same thing. I finally figured out that *you don't have to respond unless he asks three times*. It's *when he asks the third time that you can tell he cares*. And at that point, you need to answer his question. Otherwise, I threw the first two away. Don't know if it'll work for you, but it worked for me."

Following this counsel, I slunk away to my pile of requests for ancillary information on unrelated topics and threw them *all* away. Only a few of them were ever followed up on. Rarely were items requested thrice. And if my new boss did ask for things three times, I responded, because if he asked three times, he cared. He was *measuring* my response. What you measure gets done, so measure the right things.

SMART Targets Are Foundational for Feedback and Performance Management

Performance management is always measured against a target, a standard. That's what Chapter 3 was all about. Our performance expectations must be specific, measurable, attainable, relevant, and time-based. It is only *after* we clearly articulate what we want—and after we coach our followers to deliver against our expectations—that we earn the right to give feedback. And to give useful feedback, we must be a SMART ONE.

To Give Useful Feedback, Be a SMART ONE

If our targets must be SMART, our feedback on performance aimed at those targets must also be SMART.

Beyond SMART feedback, however, we must be a SMART ONE when we give the feedback. Figure 5-1 presents the SMART ONE model. Let's dissect it point by point, and you'll see how SMART targets are foundational to being a SMART ONE when giving feedback.

☞ SMART ONE: Specific

Good feedback must be *specific*. What, *specifically*, did the employee do well? The requirement for specific feedback dictates the need for specific targets—it's impossible to give specific feedback ("This isn't what I wanted!") if your initial target wasn't precise ("I'd like lunch, please").

☞ SMART ONE: Measurable

If we are to be SMART ONEs, our feedback must be *measurable*. We must—a priori—establish what will be measured, who will do the measuring, and what instrument will be authoritative ("Your watch or mine?"). Failure to be clear on the front end in expectation-setting yields conflict on the back end in immeasurable standards.

SMART ONE

S PECIFIC	**O** BJECTIVE
M EASURABLE	**N** ONTHREATENING
A CTIONABLE	**E** NCOURAGING
R ELEVANT	
T IMELY	FIGURE 5-1

☞ SMART ONE: Actionable

The feedback we give our followers must be *something they can do something about*—something they can act upon. Else why bother? So in giving someone feedback on a sales call, it might be appropriate to comment on what he or she is wearing. We can all take steps to dress appropriately for the situation. It would be less appropriate to note that the employee was "dog ugly," since most of us cannot change our physical appearance (and because employee health plans rarely cover cosmetic surgery).

☞ SMART ONE: Relevant

SMART goals must be relevant. Likewise with good feedback. The feedback must *relate* the observed behavior to its impact on previously articulated personal, work group, and corporate goals. The feedback must detail specifically how the employee helped—or blocked—the achievement of the goals.

☞ SMART ONE: Timely

Just as SMART goals must have time horizons, to be SMART ONEs, our feedback must be *timely*. It must happen immediately after the observed behavior so that the recipient associates the feedback (either positive or developmental) with the activity that produced it.

☞ SMART ONE: Objective

Good feedback is *objective*—it talks about objectively

observable behaviors that any reasonable, well-informed onlooker would see. To accomplish this objectivity, our developmental feedback must *address behaviors, not conclusions.* That is, we don't say an employee is "stupid," because that's a conclusion (and a nonobjective one, at that!). Instead we say that it has taken the employee twice as long to become half as proficient as his peers—all of whom had similar training. *It's not the stupidity we want addressed, anyhow. It's the shortfall in proficiency.*

☞ SMART ONE: Nonthreatening

Threats are designed to scare, to make afraid. People who are afraid won't move. ("He froze in terror.") So good feedback is *nonthreatening.* This is not to say it is mealy-mouthed. Good feedback is always crystal-clear about pay-offs: the carrot-rewards for on-target performance, and the stick-consequences for missing the target. We can be clear without being threatening, which is what the SMART ONEs among us do.

☞ SMART ONE: Encouraging

As SMART ONEs of the managerial world, we are *always encouraging.* We encourage those doing well to keep it up, relating continued good performance to corporate and personal payoffs. We encourage those missing the mark to get back on track by telling them why the goal is important and by revisiting the consequences for off-target performance.

It is encouragement (to continue or to change) that bridges current performance to future performance and helps employees hone in on our clearly articulated SMART performance objectives.

👍 Life Is Mostly Packaging

Life *is* mostly packaging, and nowhere is that more true than in the performance-management and feedback business. It's how we say what we say that determines how our feedback is heard.

Suppose you hear a man being described, and the description says, "He weighs over an eighth of a ton!" Contrast this with a description that says, "He weighs 253 pounds." They are both large men—no doubt about it! But the first one sounds huge. It is *packaging that makes the difference*!

Our challenge is *to package the feedback we give in a way that it has the most positive impact on the behavior of the recipient*. This is especially important when giving developmental feedback—feedback pointed at helping the employee's development by getting him to stop specific behavior or adopt more on-target behavior.

The most common—and ham-handed—approach is to lead with the negative: "You really screwed up when you did X." A more professionally packaged approach would be to lead with the positive. The feedback focuses not on the observed erroneous behavior, but on the absent—yet desired—behavior. It might be framed, "You'd be even more effective if you did Y."

Packaging feedback in this way also satisfies our commitment to be encouraging, since it calls forth from the employee behavior that will make him "more effective."

The Feedback Flowchart

Take a look at the feedback flowchart[1] shown in Figure 5-2. As you read down the decision tree, you will see that employees can give us two types of behavior: things we like and want to encourage (represented in this model by a plus sign) or things we dislike and want to discourage (represented by a minus sign). No employee behavior, however insignificant, is ever neutral. You either like it better than you dislike it, and so want to encourage it, or you dislike it more than you like it, and want to discourage it. *Every employee behavior begs for some response from a manager.*

FEEDBACK FLOWCHART

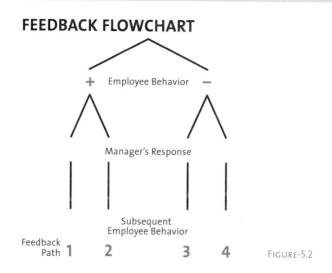

Employee Behavior

Manager's Response

Subsequent
Employee Behavior

Feedback
Path   1   2   3   4   FIGURE-5.2

Clients sometimes ask me, "But what about my 'average' employee? Is this true for them as well?" And the answer to that is probably best illustrated by an example. Consider for a moment a man with his feet in a furnace and his head in a freezer. If you measure this guy's body temperature with a rectal thermometer, on average he is comfortable. But it is a misleading average. His average "comfortable" is made up of parts of him that are miserably cold and parts that are unbearably hot.

So, too, with our average employee. That average is made up of things we admire and want to encourage (like always being at work, always having a pleasant attitude, and possessing a willingness to accept new responsibilities) combined with things we dislike and would like to discourage (a slow pace of work, low commitment to quality). Our job as managers is to encourage the things we like and extinguish the things we dislike until the employee is a top performer in *all* aspects of performance.

The best way to encourage appropriate, on-target behavior (and extinguish behavior we dislike) is through targeted, specific feedback. Intuitively, we know that it makes sense to applaud and reward the behavior we like, and to use developmental feedback to discourage undesirable behavior. Figure 5-3 fleshes out our feedback flowchart with a plus sign representing positive feedback and a minus sign representing developmental feedback.

MANAGER'S POSTIVE IMPACT

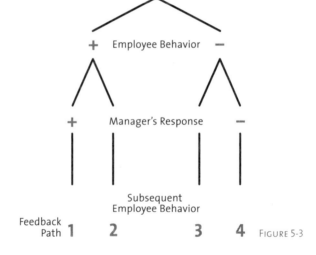

Figure 5-3

Positive Feedback *Encourages* Behavior—Developmental Feedback *Extinguishes* Behavior

The results of these managerial responses can be found at the bottom of our flowchart, shown in Figure 5-4. When specific, timely, positive feedback is attached to on-target behavior, the behavior is *encouraged*. Over time, the employee will repeat the on-target behavior more often, more completely, and to higher standards. Or, as detailed on Feedback Path 1, Figure 5-4, you will get a *stronger* positive response.

Likewise, specific, targeted developmental feedback will gradually *extinguish* the off-purpose behavior with which it is associated. Feedback Path 4 on Figure 5-4 represents this as a gradual weakening of the undesired behavior. The behavior will not turn around overnight. Most people (including me) do not work that way. But consistent, timely, specific developmental feedback will first weaken, then extinguish, behavior that is undesirable.

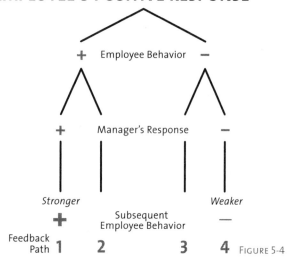

EMPLOYEE'S POSITIVE RESPONSE

FIGURE 5-4

Ignoring Good Behavior *Extinguishes* It—Ignoring Undesirable Behavior *Encourages* It

These maxims represent one of the great paradoxes of human life. They are the behavioral manifestation of a term from science: entropy. The notion of entropy holds that—left on their own—things tend to run down, decay, or fall apart. Those of us who own houses, drive cars, or live in bodies have certainly found this to be true! And it's also true for human behavior—both in the personal and the managerial realm.

There is a managerial world view that says, "It ain't my job to thank them for doing their job. I thank 'em every week when I pay 'em!" You may have heard this yourself; you may even have said it.

Likewise, there is a management mindset that says, "Look, that employee does many things right. I know he is difficult to deal with, but his productivity is high and attendance is excellent. Let's let it slide. We've got bigger fish to fry."

Both of these are examples of *ignoring* behavior that needs attention. And ultimately this will bite you on the butt.

Figure 5-5 presents a fleshed-out flowchart—with Path 2 representing ignoring good performance and Path 3 representing ignoring off-target behavior. The risk of not giving feedback on behavior—behavior of any sort—is that

MANAGER'S NEGATIVE IMPACT

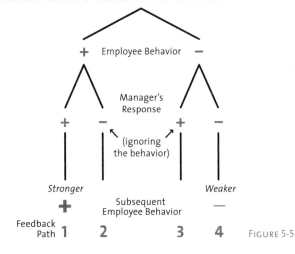

FIGURE 5-5

the employee decides that *we did not notice*. Think of the impact of being unnoticed—whether you are working hard and well, or working soft and sorry.

Figure 5-6 chases ignoring behavior to its ultimate outcome. For those who were doing good work (Feedback Path 2) they gradually begin to do less-good work. After all, why kill yourself when no one notices it? For those whose behavior is off-target (Feedback Path 3), they stray even further. After all, the boss didn't notice the first time! So, who cares?

A story: My brother-in-law is a gifted financial planner and investment counselor. He can run the numbers; he knows investments and inspires the confidence of his clients. Many years ago, he worked in the trust department of one of the country's largest banks. This was his experience.

EMPLOYEE'S NEGATIVE RESPONSE

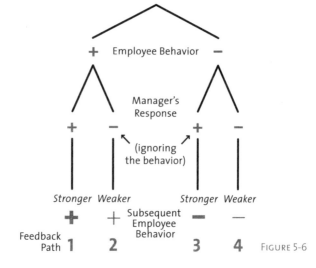

FIGURE 5-6

Carl shared an office with another investment counselor. One year Carl had a great record. His fee income was up dramatically, he beat his new account-acquisition goals, and his assets-under-management shot up. Carl was thrilled, and expected significant management recognition for his sterling performance.

Conversely, Carl's office-mate delivered wretched performance. He came late and left early, spent most of the morning reading the paper and much of the afternoon making personal phone calls. He missed all of his goals, and his assets-under-management actually *dropped* during the year.

So what happened? They got the same percentage salary increase at the end of the year! No recognition (carrots) for Carl. No developmental feedback (sticks) for his office-mate. But that's not the end of the story. Less than twelve months later, Carl left this employer, seeking a workplace that would reward good behavior with specific feedback and measurable rewards. The price of ignoring off-purpose behavior is that it gets worse. Ignoring good behavior can cost you the employee altogether!

Our job—no matter who the employee is or what the circumstance—is to identify behavior we like and give specific, targeted feedback that encourages the behavior. Simultaneously, we must pinpoint behavior that is unacceptable and encourage the employee to change the behavior. And we must—in both cases—articulate why the behavior sought is important and how on-target behavior can yield payoffs (WII-FM) for the employee.

Feedback Is a Process, Not an Event

The most difficult thing about our managerial role as feedback givers is that it is *relentless*. Like parenthood, it never stops. Every day of every week—all year long—we need to give employees feedback on what they did well, how it matters, and why it's important to keep doing it well. And we must simultaneously identify behavior that is off-target and give targeted developmental feedback that helps the employee get back on track.

In her tenure as an educator, my wife, Laura, once had the opportunity to give repeated developmental feedback to get a group of 150 students back on track. One semester she took a sabbatical to finish work on an advanced degree. When she returned to the classroom, she found that her students were cheating like bandits! They were flagrantly plagiarizing, lifting entire paragraphs from *Cliff Notes* and reference books. They were bringing cribsheets into tests, barely concealing them under their books and other papers. And they were brazenly copying from each other's work.

Obviously, the substitute who had handled Laura's class the previous semester had not painted a clear picture of the target in terms of cheating, perhaps assuming that it was unnecessary. Further, the substitute had failed to measure performance against an "honesty" standard. If students did not *re*spect her unspoken *ex*pectation of honesty, it was because she never *in*spected.

Spring semester begins, in walks Laura, and the students have a rude awakening—*no more cheating*! Laura did just the right thing: she painted a SMART picture of the target by articulating *exactly* what she meant by cheating. She held up for them the possible consequences (including a zero on the test and failure for the year) if they continued cheating, and she continued to inspect.

With this clear feedback, a couple of phone calls to parents, and some failing grades, students quickly righted their behavior, and the semester continued apace. All the students needed was developmental feedback that acknowledged their behavior and asked for something different.

How often we fail our employees in circumstances like this! We give sporadic, episodic feedback, pointed only toward astoundingly good performance or abysmally off-target behavior. Consequently, employee behavior lurches to and fro like a neophyte driver steering a car down a narrow two-lane road.

In fact, the driving metaphor is an apt one for the ongoing *process* of giving feedback. As a child I was always fascinated that—even when driving down a straight road—my mother had to continually turn the wheel slightly to stay in the middle of the lane. I now understand it: as we drive, our eyes feed back to our brains the relative position of the car vis a vis the center line on the left of our lane and the shoulder on the right. As we notice a slight drifting one way or the other, we make incremental corrections to stay on target in the center of the lane.

So it is with the *process* of managerial feedback to our employees about their performance. We give constant, ongoing feedback any time we see progression toward the target or regression away from the target. We use positive feedback to encourage the behavior we like, and developmental feedback to extinguish the behavior that is unacceptable. This helps prevent surprises at review time.

If the Employee Is Surprised at Review Time, It's *Your* Fault

Feedback is a process—regular, ongoing, specific, and pointed towards clear, SMART performance expectations. Done well—and done often—good feedback will all but eliminate those marathon, cataclysmic annual performance reviews that get blood on the walls. An annual review should contain no surprises. After all, it's a *review* of the ongoing feedback the employee has received in the process of performance management.

You Don't Have to Be Mad to Give Developmental Feedback

Somehow we have picked up the notion that we must be angry to tell someone they are missing the target. This is not true. You not only don't *have* to be angry, it *helps* to not show anger when giving developmental feedback. If we appear angry, the feedback recipient may well respond to the emotion and not the message. This will cloud the effectiveness of our developmental feedback.

Consider Laura's response to her cheating students. In point of fact, she *was* angry that her students were cheating, but she did not rant and rave; she did not fall into a tirade. She simply presented to them, as straightforwardly as possible, her expectations and the possible consequences of continued cheating, as well as a clear understanding of what constituted cheating in her mind.

They understood the facts. They understood the consequences. They knew the target. Unclouded by name-calling, finger-pointing, blaming, or shaming, they changed their behavior. Laura, as manager of the class, got what she wanted from her students—no cheating—because she was willing to give them developmental feedback.

Developmental Feedback Is an *Investment* in the Employee

Developmental feedback is hard for many managers—me included. We were socialized from an early age to be "nice." Telling someone how they are missing the target seems somehow "not nice," and we are reluctant to do it.

So here's the key question: is it nicer to tell him now, the first time you see the employee miss a performance expectation? Or is it nicer to wait, accumulate examples of his missing that target, let him "groove" the off-target behavior, and then spring the whole kit and caboodle on him at once, surprising the employee with an avalanche of developmental feedback? Which of these options is "nicer"?

It helps us give developmental feedback if we can reframe our understanding of what we are doing with the feedback. Developmental feedback is a gift—an investment, if you will, in the employee. If we split the word "developmental" we see that it helps *develop* [the] *mental* abilities of the employee to do things well. And that—after all—is one of *our* key accountabilities as managers.

Think for a moment about Laura's high school classes. These students were college-bound the year after they were in Laura's class. Her clear articulation of the expectation of honesty—and her willingness to hold them in account for their own honesty—prepared them for the environment they would encounter in college. It also likely prevented some of them from having an early and painful exit from the college of their choice!

Laura invested in these students by the precision and candor of her developmental feedback, and that is the only reason for developmental feedback. *The focus is not to punish; the focus is to get the employee back on track.* As managers, we are paid for marshalling limited human, financial, and mechanical resources, and applying these resources to seemingly unlimited tasks. Screaming at the human resources *does not* incline them to work harder to reach our SMART goals.

However, resetting the goal, painting a clear picture of the target, articulating consequences or potential rewards, and talking about the "whys" *does* encourage people to work harder to reach SMART goals. And that's what Laura was doing with her investment of developmental feedback when she encountered her English students during their cheating epidemic.

I'm Not Here to Prosecute the Guilty, I'm Here to Solve the Problem

I first heard this maxim over twenty years ago while working with Robert Smith at Reynolds Tobacco Company. Robert entered someone's office seeking corrections for a computer printout. As Robert made his request, he was hit with a barrage of explanations, excuses, and exceptions, the general tone of which was, "*My people could not have possibly made that mistake, and don't pick on us!*"

Robert listened to this barrage for a minute. He then responded as coolly as I have ever heard anyone respond, "But you don't understand. I'm not here to prosecute the guilty, I'm here to solve the problem." And solve the problem he did. With that entrée, the co-worker was willing to hear Robert's developmental feedback and partner with him to solve the problem.

As we have observed, life is mostly packaging. By packaging his request for a new report in a nonthreatening and conciliatory way, Robert got the information he needed and was able to move forward. That is the outcome we seek every time we give feedback to those with whom we work, whether they are our subordinates, superiors, colleagues, or people who exist in our social and familial worlds.

You have to earn the right to give feedback and manage performance. You earn that right by assessing your employee's key motivators, by defining and communicating SMART targets, and by COACHing well. But all the above is useless without specific, on-target feedback—both positive and developmental—pointed at eliciting bulls-eye performance from your employees.

MAXIMS ON FEEDBACK AND PERFORMANCE MANAGEMENT

People will *re*spect what you *ex*pect if you *in*spect.

What you count is what you get, so count the right things.

Don't confuse motion with progress.

SMART targets are foundational for feedback and performance management.

To give useful feedback, be a SMART ONE.

Life is mostly packaging.

Positive feedback *encourages* behavior—Developmental feedback *extinguishes* behavior.

Ignoring good behavior *extinguishes* it—Ignoring negative behavior *encourages* it.

Feedback is a process, not an event.

If the employee is surprised at review time, it's *your* fault.

You don't have to be mad to give developmental feedback.

Developmental feedback is an *investment* in the employee.

I'm not here to prosecute the guilty, I'm here to solve the problem.

QUESTIONS FOR REFLECTION

1. Have you ever painted someone a clear picture of your *expectation*, then fallen short on *inspection*? What happened? Did your employee *respect* your expectation?

2. Have you ever "counted the wrong things"? What happened? How long did it take you to realize your mistake?

3. Referring to the feedback flowchart in Figure 5-6, which feedback path do you do better, 1 or 4? Where do you make the most mistakes, 2 or 3?

4. Do *you* have to be mad to give developmental feedback? Why did you answer as you did?

CHALLENGE FOR APPLICATION

Think of a person you oversee who is not performing as well as you would like. What's going on here? How can you use positive and developmental feedback to enhance his/her performance? Have you been ignoring behavior that you should acknowledge? What is your plan?

6

REWARDS AND CONSEQUENCES

Now we've come to money time—literally and figuratively. We're talking about rewards and consequences—the carrots and sticks of our Chapter 2 motivational model.

All our work thus far has been leading up to this point. We began with a vision and reduced our vision to a cogent plan. We thought about our team and assessed how to motivate each team member. We painted a clear picture of our SMART target and coached our employees on how to hit it. And we gave feedback—both positive and developmental—as employees moved toward the target. Now it's payoff time—time for employees to reap what they have sown, to gather the rewards of on-target, purposeful behavior or to feel the consequences of repeated behavior that has missed the mark.

The process of handing out rewards and consequences is derived from combining two of our previous chapters—Motivation (Chapter 2) and Feedback and Performance

Management (Chapter 5). For, in shaping rewards and consequences, we are giving tangible feedback with which we hope to engender motivation. It's as simple—and as difficult—as that.

Different Things Have to Happen to Good Performers vs. Poor Performers

Remember our story from the previous chapter about Carl, the investment counselor? It is astounding how often managers in America will manage to the lowest acceptable level of performance. In effect, these managers punish the employees, like Carl, who have worked the hardest and been the most successful. Although these employees wind up doing most of the work, the manager rewards all employees with the same reward at the end of the day. In the first place, it's patently unfair. It's also lazy, a fruit of managers who aren't diligent enough to separate the wheat from the chaff. And it's woefully ineffective as a managerial strategy, because there is no effective "sort" saying, "This is good, keep doing it," or "This is undesirable, knock it off."

People-management seems to be one of the few places where we are afraid to share different rewards for high, versus low, performers. The stock market, in contrast, assigns the highest price/earnings multiples to corporations (and business sectors) that either (1) have performed well in the past, or (2) are expected to perform well in the future.

Likewise, the world of collegiate and professional athletics provides very different rewards to winning coaches than to losing coaches. The same is true for winning, versus losing, players.

The strangest thing about our reluctance to identify and recognize high performers is this: *everybody already knows who they are anyway.* Ask any group who among them is best at their assigned task and they will tell you. They already know. Yet we are reluctant to single out high performers or to call low performers into account. And that is too bad.

For years, child-development psychologists have told us that children and young adults, no matter how they bristle against them, hunger for rules and guidelines and some notion of what constitutes "good" behavior from the parental viewpoint. Beyond the rules themselves, young people long to see the rules *enforced*, and to know that there are certain points beyond which they simply cannot go. Certain things they cannot do. And, that different things will happen to them when they comply with the rules than when they don't.

It is exactly the same with our employees. The best way to get good performance is to recognize good performance. The best way to ensure mediocre performance is to pay attention only to the folks who are worse than mediocre.

Pay Attention to the Middle

Remember when you were in elementary school? Which students did *all* the teachers know? They knew the students who were *really* bright, the students who needed more help, and the students who behaved badly. And the vast middle remained a faceless crowd. Don't make this same mistake with those you manage. Always be on the lookout for any *positive behavior* you want to *encourage*—from even your most-average employee. And always identify *off-target behavior* the first time you see it, and offer *developmental feedback* to *extinguish* it.

Bad News Ages Poorly

We want to identify off-target behavior and intervene immediately because *bad news ages poorly*. The bad news in this case is two-fold: (1) the employee is missing the target, and (2) you've caught 'em.

Further, as an employee continues to do something wrong over and over, she begins to "groove" the off-purpose behavior. And the longer she does it wrong, the harder it will be to right the behavior when you finally do intervene. (For those who play golf or tennis, it's akin to trying to fix your backswing or your serve after years of consistently doing it the same, wrong way.)

Our task is to offer rewards that consistently pull superior performance out of employees, and to introduce consequences that the employees do not want to experience.

Pay Off in Currency That Matters to the Employee

Suppose you run a gas station in rural North Carolina. In drives a long, green Jaguar, and a sporty gentleman pops out and says, "I say, old chap, would you happen to have some petrol?" He fills up the tank, then strides in to pay the tab, handing you the weirdest looking currency you've ever seen. "What's this?" you ask. "Why those, my good man, are British pounds," comes the reply.

Now you know you've got a problem. This isn't Great Britain, and you want $23.75 in American greenbacks, or you are going to fetch the siphon hose. What's the problem? He didn't pay off in currency that mattered to you.

One of our major jobs as managers is to pay off in currency that matters to the employee we are trying to motivate. That is, for each employee, we have to offer rewards he or she wants to receive, and dangle consequences she or he wants to avoid. What matters most is the attractiveness of the rewards (and repulsiveness of the consequences) *to the employee, not to us.*

In our chapter on motivation, we explored the notion that, "If we listen long enough, people will tell us how to motivate them." And this is the place that aphorism really comes into play. Motivation is a unique and individual thing—different from person to person, and different from day to day for the same person. I once had the opportunity to play a board game called Therapy with some close friends of mine. In this game, people play in pairs, with one person (the therapist) trying to correctly forecast the answer of his teammate (the client) to a variety of questions. A correct answer allows the team to advance its token (a small couch) around the board.

During the course of the game, one player drew a card that asked "Which would you rather do, (1) eat a meal in a fine restaurant, (2) go on an unlimited shopping spree, or (3) have delirious, delicious sex?"

The player responded, "I don't know, it would depend on what I did last!"

In many ways, the choice of motivators *does* depend on what the person did last. And our job as managers is to make sure that—having listened long enough—we select the motivators that will work with *this* employee, *this* time, in *these* circumstances. To do this well, we must suspend our tendency to judge, and *really listen* to our employees as they articulate *their motivators*.

It's Not Our Job to Make Value Judgments about Our Employees' Motivators

As managers, it shouldn't matter to us *what* matters to the employees. It's not our job to make value judgments about our employees' motivators. It's our job to ferret out, to understand, and to respond to that understanding by offering employees the payoffs they seek as motivators. (Or the consequences they most *don't* want to experience!)

Several years ago I assumed new responsibilities in the company where I was working. Among the responsibilities was the supervision of a professionally trained engineer who was now serving in a sales management position.

I sat down to get to know this person better, and asked him to tell me about the single achievement he was most proud of in his life. I don't know what I expected, but here's what I got.

He said, "I'm proud that I have built a successful career and now have a prestige car and live in a high-status neighborhood. I can wear tailored suits and a brand-name, high-status watch. I'm a big deal, and I like it!"

This employee gave me exactly what I asked for. He told me precisely how (money, material rewards) to motivate him. Unfortunately, I was operating from a managerial place that *judged his motivators rather than using his motivational profile to get superior performance from him.*

My values and motivational profile got in the way of successfully managing this employee. I offered him the things that would motivate *me* (a chance to play on a winning team and to do something that mattered), and he sat there, inert, because I wasn't listening.

Had I offered this employee money, status, and power, he would have worked tirelessly to get those rewards, because they were rewards he cared about. Instead, I assumed he "was raised at my house" and offered the rewards that motivate me. He wasn't. And they didn't.

My stubbornness and my unwillingness to meet this employee's needs cost me his enthusiasm, and a good employee for six months. That's a lot of wasted time to result from nothing but managerial obstinance!

Match the Magnitude of the Payoffs—or the Consequences—to the Magnitude of the Performance

What does this mean? It means that payoffs—or consequences—should be commensurate with performance. An example: you have an employee who has been doing below-average work for several weeks. You have coached and counseled her, and she promises improvement.

The next week you notice that her work—while still not excellent—has improved markedly.

If you want the improvement to be permanent, you must acknowledge it. This way the employee can tell that you know the difference between good and bad performance.

You don't have to give her a raise; you don't have to have a brass band playing; you don't have to recognize her at the next employee meeting. And you certainly don't have to promote her. You *do* have to acknowledge it to her, though, if you want to continue seeing the improved performance you just observed.

Similarly, suppose you have a generally good employee whose performance suddenly falls off. Not dramatically, but noticeably. You don't want to scream and yell at him, and you certainly don't want to lose him. (Who among us has enough "generally good" employees?) You must shape a consequence—given his motivational profile—that is commensurate with the diminished performance level. Otherwise, the employee's behavior will continue to disintegrate.

> ## Ignoring Improvement in Performance Will Extinguish It— Ignoring Slippage in Performance Will Encourage It

These two maxims are adapted from our earlier chapter on feedback and performance management (Chapter 5). The differences are subtle but important. Our job as managers is to *recognize any changes in performance and respond to them quickly and appropriately.* The changes (and the related rewards and consequences) do not have to be enormous to be important. Any time there is change, we must recognize it, and *make sure our employees know that we know the difference.*

An example might help, though you've likely experienced both of these maxims in your own work life. Let's say you have two employees: Mike and Ike.

Mike is the perfect employee—he does good-quality work and lots of it. He arrives early and stays until the job is complete. In the past he has regularly exceeded your expectations for quality and quantity of work. In the last week, though, you've noticed his quality index has fallen slightly and his productivity is off as well.

Ike, on the other hand, sets low standards and regularly fails to meet them. His work—what there is of it—is adequate but not outstanding. He is often tardy and has several unexplained absences per pay period. Yet over the last two weeks he has been on time, every time. Even his production level is up.

Now here is one of the great perversities of life: ignore Ike's improved performance—by not thanking him, or providing opportunities for growth, *or recognizing him in some way that matters to him*—and his work quality and enthusiasm will soon be extinguished. Because *he will think you can't tell the difference*. How could he know you've noticed? You've never told him.

But ignore Mike's slumping performance and you'll get more of it. He, too, will think you can't tell the difference. And *the lowest acceptable level of work will prevail.*

Neither of these changes in performance is epic or cataclysmic. Ike certainly does not get a promotion for showing up on time two weeks in a row. And we don't push an employee overboard for a brief slippage in performance. But *both changes in performance cry out for appropriate, commensurate recognition.*

Our job as managers is to work both sides of this perverse model. We recognize improved achievement to encourage continued improvement—to *let them know we can tell the difference*. And we call slipping performers into account, so they will fix the problem. We want them, also, *to know we can tell the difference*. Ignoring sub-par performance is not an option. If you ignore it, it will *not* go away.

The *best time* to give anyone feedback on changed performance is the *first time* you observe the change.

Just Do It—*NOW!*

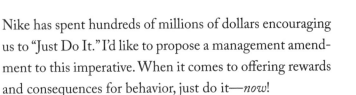

Nike has spent hundreds of millions of dollars encouraging us to "Just Do It." I'd like to propose a management amendment to this imperative. When it comes to offering rewards and consequences for behavior, just do it—*now!*

The *very best time to give people payoffs*—whether rewards or consequences—is *immediately upon observing the behavior* you want to encourage or extinguish. There is no better time to provide appropriate payoffs than when a person has just accomplished something you want to reward, or when a person has just missed a target that you want to call to their attention. *Give the payoff immediately* so that it will be associated with the behavior you just observed.

Within limits, beware of offering significant payoffs solely for effort. Trying is important. Little of any worth is ever accomplished without effort. But *trying* is not the goal. *Doing* (successfully, on-target, within budget, to specs) is the goal.

If effort—rather than output—is rewarded, then effort is what you'll get. (Remember: what you reward is what you get!) The manager's task is to applaud effort, while continuing to point employees to the ultimate goal: output. The same goes for motion versus progress. It requires motion to generate progress. But the presence of motion does not, perforce, mean progress is taking place. So *associate the rewards and consequences you offer with the ultimate outcome you seek*. And if you're not getting results, take a hard look at the reward-consequence pattern you are using.

For Different Results, Change the Pattern

A famous mental health expert once commented, "If you keep doing what you've been doing and expect different results—that's insanity." And it's the kind of insanity I often see at work in the management of people. If what you're doing isn't working, change the pattern!

You've ignored sub-par performance, hoping it will go away? It hasn't worked? Change the pattern!

You've fed carrots to this employee over and over again? It hasn't worked? Change the pattern!

You've talked only about consequences with a sub-par employee? It hasn't worked? Change the pattern!

We must monitor what we've been doing in terms of feedback and rewards and consequences. If it's working, we continue it. If it's not, we must tweak it. If you keep doing what you've been doing, you'll keep getting what you've been getting. For different results, change the pattern.

> # In General, People Change Behavior When the Pain of Changing Is Less Than the Pain of Staying the Same *or* When the Joy of Changing Is Greater Than the Joy of Staying the Same

Rewards and consequences are all about change—about encouraging people to change behavior that misses the mark, and to continue changes that take them closer to the mark. And change is hard, hard work.

Our task as managers is to *make the rewards of change so great that our employees can't resist.* And to *make the consequences of not changing so severe that our employees want to change.* Either payoff—rewards or consequences—will work.

Reflect for a moment on someone who is profoundly addicted—to alcohol or drugs, perhaps. He loses his job, but it has no impact on his behavior. Then he loses his family. Again no impact. His home. No impact. His car. No impact. And then, one day, our protagonist wakes up, shivering, under a bridge. He is cold and wet and hungry, and he sees the ultimate consequence of continuing to live this way: death. He has "hit bottom" in the language of recovery. Suddenly, the consequences of continued off-target behavior are clear to him. He forswears his addiction and begins the long road to recovery. Confronting severe consequences, in this case, created the impetus for change. Or, in the words of our maxim, he changed because "the pain of changing was less than the pain of staying the same."

Now consider a happier scenario. A bright, young college graduate is about to enter an MBA program. He is single and has enjoyed the single life. There are several women in his life but no serious girlfriends. And then he meets someone who is just a little different.

She is, perhaps, not like the other women he has known. She has mettle—a quiet but steely resolve that is best not tampered with. She is independent without being a lone wolf, loving without being smothering. And our bright, carefree young man finds his world turned upside down.

He proposes. She accepts. Eight weeks later, they are wed. What happened? "The joy of changing (marital status) was greater than the joy of staying the same."

Managers have many key accountabilities: painting SMART targets, COACHing, giving specific targeted feedback. None of these is more important than the charge to ensure that different things happen to good performers versus poor performers by paying off in currency that matters to the employee. If you're not getting what you want, make sure your reward and consequence patterns are reinforcing appropriate—or discouraging inappropriate—behaviors from your employees. Tweak that reward/consequence pattern so that you *do something different to engender different results.*

MAXIMS ON REWARDS AND CONSEQUENCES

Different things have to happen to good performers versus poor performers.

Pay attention to the middle.

Bad news ages poorly.

Pay off in currency that matters to the employee.

It's not our job to make value judgments about our employees' motivators.

Match the magnitude of the payoffs—or consequences—to the magnitude of the performance.

Ignoring improvement in performance will extinguish it.

Ignoring slippage in performance will encourage it.

Just do it—*NOW*!

For different results, change the pattern.

In general, people change behavior when the pain of changing is less than the pain of staying the same *or* when the joy of changing is greater than the joy of staying the same.

QUESTIONS FOR REFLECTION

1. Have you ever worked in a place where good performers and poor performers received the same reward? What impact did this have on your performance?

2. Why is it so hard to "pay attention to the middle"? What can you do to ensure that you attend to the middle in your organization?

3. Have you ever made value judgments about an employee's motivators? How did it hamper your ability to manage him well?

4. For different results, change the pattern. From whom in your work team are you getting sub-par results? How might you change the pattern?

CHALLENGE FOR APPLICATION

Pay off in currency that matters to your employees. What currencies have you found most useful in motivating yourself? Your employees? (Figures 2-3 and 2-4 in Chapter 2 may help you flesh out your lists.) How can you make sure you listen to your employees so that you can learn the rewards and consequences that matter to them?

7

RELATIONSHIP MANAGEMENT

Everyone Is Keeping Score, and That's Okay

"Everyone is keeping score, and that's okay." This is a statement you don't often hear, and it's anathema to many people when they do hear it. But it's also true, and the truth of the statement is easy to validate in our experience of everyday life. Let's look at a couple of examples.

Think for a moment about your most recent trip down the interstate highway. You are cruising along at 75 miles an hour, and suddenly you notice brake lights ahead. You begin to decelerate, and soon you are stuck in stop-and-roll traffic, going 3 miles per hour. Gradually you creep under an overpass, and on the other side of the overpass you realize traffic is backed all the way up the on-ramp. As you approach the stalled ramp traffic, the person at the head of the line begs you—with clenched hands and a prayerful gesture—to let him in. You grudgingly acquiesce, and wave him into the creeping line of traffic in front of you. As you motion him in, he merges slowly into the traffic right in front of you and moves on down the road.

What do you expect from the driver of the other car in this situation? You have just *invested* in him; he has received something from you. What are your expectations from him? You expect him to wave—to acknowledge, somehow, the sacrifice you have made on his behalf, the gift you have given him. If he waves, the transaction is complete and you both go on about your business, likely never to see each other again. If he doesn't wave or nod his thanks, you fume. "Why, I let that stupid bozo into this traffic, and he didn't even acknowledge me!"

Everybody is keeping score, and that's okay.

There's nothing inherently wrong in keeping score. This second story illustrates scorekeeping in a kinder, gentler context. You and your significant other receive a social invitation from some good friends of yours. You go, have a good time, enjoy their company, and return home glowing with memories of the happy occasion. The next day you call to thank them, and make a mental note that sooner or later you *must* have this couple to your house.

Time goes by, they have not yet visited your house, and they call again, this time with tickets to a professional sporting event. You and your beloved go, once again have a good time, enjoy their company, and return home, talking the entire way about the *imperative* need to reciprocate the invitation. Though you call with profuse thanks for their ongoing hospitality, your professional lives are busy, and several weeks elapse without your reciprocating *either* of the invitations your friends have extended.

Lo and behold, they call a third time—this time with tickets to the theater and an invitation to supper at one of the finest restaurants in town. As their third gracious invitation is communicated, you ask them to hold on just a minute, and frantically cover the mouthpiece of the telephone with your hand. "Honey, this is the Joneses again!" you holler. "They want us to come with them to dinner and the theater! We can't do that—it's *our* turn to have them over *here*."

Everybody is keeping score, and that's okay.

But if everybody is keeping score, how do we know what the score is? How do we track the score in our relationships in a way that is useful and contributes to the health of the relationships? I have found it helpful to imagine each of my relationships like a piggybank: I envision each interaction with a person as either adding to, or subtracting from, the balance in the piggybank.

In teaching this concept in my training workshops, I often ask participants, "How are relationships like piggybanks?" They have fun chasing this idea, and the insights are myriad. Figure 7-1 presents some of the similarities between relationships and piggybanks.

PIGGYBANKS AND RELATIONSHIPS

- It takes a long time to build a balance.

- We invest now for a payoff in the future.

- You have to make an investment before you can make a withdrawal.

- You only get out of it what you put in it.

- Sometimes you can't get out as much as you have put in.

- It's possible—with relationships and with piggybanks—to bust them wide open.

- Once busted open, both are difficult to repair.

- Investments (and withdrawals) can be in different amounts—and even in different currencies.

FIGURE 7-1

The last of the insights on Figure 7-1 is a key one: "Investments (and withdrawals) can be in different amounts—and even in different currencies." This is particularly important for those of us who are interested in management. If "everyone is keeping score," then how do we know the best way to score more points with a particular employee? What is the right currency, the appropriate denomination?

This chapter presents several tools that will help you know what the score is with your employees. As you reflect on these tools, remember that there is no universal "employee." Employees are single, individual, living, breathing entities. Our task is to know and respond to them individually.

Use the Relationship Ledger to Know the Score

One disciplined way to think about your employee relationships is to visualize each employee as a separate account—with its own ledger sheet for recording transactions. Some transactions (a raise, recognition for a job well done) are almost universally considered investments in an employee's account. Other transactions (a public flogging for a minor mistake) are almost always withdrawals. Figure 7-2 fleshes out the ledger-sheet concept.

What Is an Investment to One Employee Can Be a Withdrawal to Another

The difficult thing about knowing how to invest in any *particular* employee is that *what is an investment to one employee can be a withdrawal to another*.

I once visited with a high-level executive at Wachovia Bank—a multistate bank holding company. I asked him what he liked best about his work at Wachovia, expecting

RELATIONSHIPS AS LEDGERS

MANAGER: Rhoda Block
EMPLOYEE: Lane Closure

INVESTMENTS—CREDITS	WITHDRAWALS—DEBITS
+	**−**
• 12% raise	• Public flogging for a minor mistake
• Recognition for a job well done	• Having suggestions rejected without a fair hearing
• Being authentically listened to by the manager	• Absence of items in the investment column
• Have input into tasks (selection and manner of completion)	
• Having clear, SMART targets from the manager	

FIGURE 7-2

an answer about the challenge, the pace, or his stature in the corporation and the community.

His response was a simple four-word phrase: "They leave me alone!" So, a key reward for this executive was autonomy. He saw being left alone as a major plus.

Another employee might experience being left alone in a very different way. Remember Don from Chapter 2? Leave him alone and he sulks! Being left alone is an investment for the Wachovia executive and a withdrawal for Don.

Our task is to manage our employee relationships in a way that the investments we give each employee are ones that matter to him. Further, we want to eliminate—or at least *minimize*—any withdrawals from our employee accounts.

Absent Any Other Information, Assume Your Employee Is a Carrot Person

We've talked about the dangers of *assuming*. Everyone, after all, wasn't raised at our house. Still, we often face new relationships with employees we have never met before. How should we proceed?

We should proceed by getting to know them as well—and as quickly—as possible. And in the interim, we should operate on the assumption that they are carrot people. My own experience tells me that most people—most of the time—work to embrace pleasure (eat carrots) rather than to avoid pain (avoid sticks).

While each person has their own unique investment and motivational profile, some universal investments can be assumed. Few people respond negatively to recognition for a job well done, or to being authentically listened to, or to having a say in the tasks they do and the manner in which they do them. So, as an initial operating assumption, you can assume each new employee with whom you work is a carrot person.

If You Listen Long Enough, People Will Tell You How to Invest in (Motivate) Them

There is no need, however, to proceed for long on your initial operating assumption. Set aside time to sit down with your employee and really *hear* her. That alone will be more investment than she has received from some previous managers! *Listen* as she tells you what matters to her, how she likes to be motivated, what her aspirations and goals and hopes are. Then tailor your management-relationship style to incorporate what you have learned.

It's the Manager's Job to Make the First Investment in a Professional Relationship

How many times has an insurance agent called and offered to take you to lunch? Why do they *do* that? They do it because taking you to lunch is an *investment*; the agent hopes that buying you lunch will build the balance in his account, and that you will ultimately bring the account book into balance by buying insurance from him. It's not a strict quid pro quo, and neither party expects it to be. But if you accept four lunches and never buy insurance, you can bet the lunch invitations will stop. The relationship will be out of balance.

Our job as manager is to make the first investment in our accounts with our employees. We invest by listening, by painting clear pictures of the target, and by doing unto them as they would like to be done unto. Then we ask them to repay our investment with high-quality productive output targeted at our SMART performance expectations.

When what we expect and what we get are the same thing, we're happy and the sailing is smooth on our untroubled managerial waters. And likewise for employees: it's not hard to be happy when you are getting what you want. Would that life was always so easy!

When Expectations and Reality Are Not Equal, Stress Is Created

The Stress-Creation Model (Figure 7-3) presents a simple understanding of the primary source of the stress that can occur in human relationships. Taking a look at the model, we can see that *stress is created whenever expectations and*

STRESS-CREATION MODEL

EXPECTATIONS ≠ REALITY

You only have three options:

- Change expectations (whatcha want)
- Change reality (whatcha got)
- Live in the stress

FIGURE 7-3

reality are out of congruence. That is, we become stressed whenever we want something and don't get it. Likewise, we are stressed when we get something we don't want.

Let's examine this model in the real world, and see if we can hang some flesh on these bones. You wake up one fine spring morning, bright-eyed, bushy-tailed, and ready to go to work. You bound out of bed, pop into the bathroom, and turn on the shower.

There's no hot water. So you start your day with a cold shower. Being the resilient person that you are, you weather this storm and head downstairs for breakfast—only to find that there's no coffee.

So, on this day when you had to take a cold shower, you now have breakfast without your morning caffeine quota. And this is too bad, because you're *cold*, and you had planned to drink one cup of coffee, then pour a second into your shoes to warm your feet!

Irritated but undaunted, you bound down the back steps, briefcase in hand, ready to face whatever trials the working world can throw your way. As you approach your car, you notice that it is canted a little bit to the left. When you walk around to the driver's side, you see why: the left front tire is flat.

You are beginning to get a flavor of what kind of day this is going to be. You're not even into traffic yet, and *three of your expectations* for the day *have already gone unmet.* You have not had a warm shower, your morning has been coffee-less, and now, you're jacking up the front of your car to change a tire. Clearly, your day is off to a bad start and you are living in Stressville. All of this stress is a simple result of the fact that what you wanted (a hot shower, a cup of coffee, a car with four usable tires) is not what you have. You are stressed because *your expectations and your reality are out of congruence.*

Glance for a moment at Figure 7-3, and you can see that there are only three options available to us when our expectations and our reality are not congruent. We can change our expectations, we can change our reality, or we can live in the tension of expectations unmet by reality.

Let's reflect on that cold shower as a way of looking at the options available any time we are stressed. You pop out of bed, turn on the shower, and realize you have no hot water. You're stressed; you want hot water. Now let's take a look at the options.

You can change what you *want.* You can change your *expectations.* You can decide that you want a cold shower. (It's not the choice I'd make, but I know some who have made it.)

You could also change what you've *got.* You could change your *reality.* You can call a friend, see if they have hot water, grab your toilet articles and towel, and bop over to their house to take a shower. It's not particularly convenient, but it's certainly warmer than the goose-bump option.

Or—the third option—you could *live in the tension*. You could resign yourself to the fact that *this* morning you will take a cold shower, though it is not your preference. You can realize that *this* day, in *these* circumstances, the better choice is to suffer this indignity quickly, get on with life, and have a plumber over before it's time to take another shower.

These are your options—and your only options—if you're going to take a shower at all. Any of these options will work if you can accept the consequences.

A hot shower is not an item of epic importance in our lives. On items of more consequence, however, the third option (living in the tension) is often not a wise choice. It is hard for us to live continuously in the tension of unmet expectations without going ballistic. My general experience is that, when we "live in the tension" about things that matter to us, sooner or later there will be an explosion.

The seed of this reality is captured in a quote from the former dean of the Wake Forest University Graduate School of Business. His name was Frank Schilagi, and he was a rare combination of earned academic credentials and tremendous success in the world of practical commerce.

During the first semester of my tenure in business school, Dr. Schilagi taught a class on power and failure. Early in the class, he told us, "Any time you make false expectations of others—or allow others to make false expectations of you—you are laying the groundwork for future confrontation." I have observed this to be true—both for myself and for my clients, and it informs my caution against option three, "living in the stress."

When we have expectations that go unmet, something has to happen to our stress. If we change neither the expectation nor the reality, we just bank the stress. Sooner or later, we get a tremendous return on our invested stress, which often pays off in a cataclysmic confrontation. Our task—as people who value relationships and who want to manage the balance in our relationships—is to understand fully the balances we are carrying in these relationships, and to *make sure that* (for both ourselves and our colleagues) *the expectations and the reality are congruent.*

Periodic Relationship Audits Can Identify the Stress Caused by Divergent Expectations

The best way to ensure congruence in our relationships is through the relationship audit. You'll see the relationship audit[1] detailed in Figure 7-4. It is a simple, two-by-two matrix. In the left column it measures expectations, in the right column, realities. The top row measures expectations and realities for the *employee*, and the bottom row measures *our* expectations and realities as managers in relationship to the employee.

The relationship audit can provide a powerful reality check for us in understanding the current balance in our managerial relationships. It can also provide a useful springboard for discussion when we audit relationships with those we manage. Relationships are most healthy and in best balance when three things occur: (1) the expectations of the employee equal the employee's perceived reality; (2) our (the manager's) expectations and reality are in balance; and (3) the employee and the manager have a full, mutual understanding of each other's expectations.

Looking at Figure 7-5, you will see that the only way we can fully understand anothers' expectations and perceptions

	Expectations Column	Reality Column
Employee's Worldview	What does this employee EXPECT FROM ME as a manager?	What is this employee ACTUALLY GETTING FROM ME as a manager?
Manager's (our) Worldview	What do I EXPECT from this employee?	What am I ACTUALLY GETTING from this employee?

FIGURE 7-4

is to *ask* them. We must ask the employee to clearly articulate his expectations and the reality he is experiencing. We can try to back up from the relationship far enough to reflect on our employee's understanding of *our* management actions, but we can never fully know another's perceptions unless they tell us point-blank.

In the area below the dotted line, on Figure 7-5, we must be very precise with ourselves about both our expectations and the reality we are experiencing. This is a useful exercise to complete *before* we discuss our frustration at unmet expectations with another person. I have found that I often walk around with a vague sense of unease, grumbling to myself about someone's unfairness or lack of appreciation for me. But I never fully articulate—to myself let alone to him— what it is he has done or not done that leaves me unhappy.

	Expectations Column	Reality Column
Employee's Worldview	What does this employee EXPECT FROM ME as a manager? (Though we can guess, to fully understand the employee's expectations we must ASK FOR THEM!)	What is this employee ACTUALLY GETTING FROM ME as a manager? (Though we can guess, to fully understand the employee's reality we must ASK FOR THEM!)
Manager's (our) Worldview	What do I EXPECT from this employee?	What am I ACTUALLY GETTING from this employee?

FIGURE 7-5

The relationship audit can be a tool that disciplines me to think clearly about how the other has let me down. It also forces me to examine my expectations of the other person before I enter with them into the "future confrontation" of which Dr. Schilagi spoke. We all enter relationships with unspoken expectations—some of which we have not acknowledged even to ourselves. Nowhere is that more true than marriage. Here is a story about a place where the relationship audit would have been very helpful to me as a newlywed.

My wife's father can fix *anything*. He can wire and weld. He can plumb, fell trees, and do finished carpentry. He can landscape and do automotive repairs. So who do you think fixed things at Laura's house when she was growing up? And who do you think *she expected* to fix things after she was married?

At my house, the story was different. My father is quite adept with tools—he even wired the second story of my childhood home. But it was my mother who repaired the things that broke. She can't fix anything herself, but she's got a calendar, a list, a phone book, and a checkbook, and she'll call someone till she gets it fixed! So who do you think *I expected* to fix things?

So into married life we sailed. All was fine for a couple of years, 'cause we didn't *own* anything. We lived in a furnished attic apartment—if things broke, we just told the landlady. Then we moved to our own home and reaped the "future confrontation" of our unarticulated expectations.

Something would break. Laura would circle the broken item, muttering under her breath: "When's he going to get it fixed? It's been two weeks. It's the man's job to fix stuff! Why doesn't he get on the ball!?"

And there I came, not far behind her, lip poked out, grumbling, "Doggonit, sink's been leaking for two weeks. When's she gonna call the plumber? It's the woman's job to get it scheduled. She hasn't done a thing!"

After dozens of iterations, Laura and I finally figured out what was going on. But it sure would have been helpful to start out with the relationship audit—a tool that would have driven us each to be specific about *our expectations*, and about *reality as we experienced it*.

Everybody is keeping score, and that's okay. Given that this is true, there are tools that can help us be more effective as we relate to those we manage. We've looked at three of them here in Chapter 7.

First, we examined the relationship ledger, realizing that all healthy relationships are based on an ongoing pattern of investments and withdrawals by both parties in the relationship. We then moved to the stress-creation model, a model that helps us understand what creates stress (when expectations and reality are incongruent) and our three options when these circumstances occur (we can change what we want, we can change what we've got, or we can live in the tension).

Finally, we took a close look at a simple but powerful

tool that will help us understand the nature of our managerial relationships; a tool that can help us identify possible sources of conflict when we—or the other person—begin to feel stressed in the relationship. The relationship audit allows us to look at expectations and realities for both ourselves and the other person in the relationship. In doing this, we come to a much clearer understanding—a "map" if you will—of the relationship.

These simple but effective tools will leave us with a much better understanding of the "score" in the managerial relationships we have, and will help clarify for us changes we need to make when we find our work relationships out of balance.

⚔ MAXIMS ON RELATIONSHIP ⚔ MANAGEMENT

Everybody is keeping score, and that's okay.

Use the relationship ledger to know the score.

What is an investment to one employee can be a withdrawal to another.

Absent any other information, assume your employee is a carrot person.

If you listen long enough, people will tell you how to invest in (motivate) them.

It's the manager's job to make the first investment in a professional relationship.

When expectations and reality are not equal, stress is created.

Anytime you make false expectations of others—or allow others to make false expectations of you—you are laying the groundwork for future confrontation.

Periodic relationship audits can identify the stress caused by divergent expectations.

QUESTIONS FOR REFLECTION

1. What is your initial reaction to the notion that "everyone is keeping score"? Do you believe it? Why or why not?

2. What are some specific ways you—as a manager— can make the first investment in the employees you manage?

3. Think of a time you were profoundly stressed. What was your expectation? How did the reality you experienced diverge from your expectation? How did you resolve it?

4. Have you ever "made false expectations of others"? Have you allowed others to "make false expectations of you"? What was the outcome?

CHALLENGE FOR APPLICATION

Think about a business colleague with whom you have had a rocky relationship in the past. What did he expect of you? What did you expect of him? What were your relationship realities? How could you have used the relationship audit to be clear with each other (paint a SMART target of expectations) so that you two could have had a fighting chance of not fighting?

8

SELF-MANAGEMENT: THE TOUGHEST NUT OF ALL

Self-management *is* the toughest nut of all. It's hard to manage yourself, because you are so intimately bound up with yourself. You are prone—on the one hand—to *forgive yourself offenses you would never accept in other people.* And you're prone—on the other hand—to *hold yourself to impossibly high standards that no one could ever reach.*

Both of these excesses—the excess of impossibly high standards and the excess of cheap forgiveness—make managing ourselves the most difficult task we will ever confront, in business or in life. Still, it must be done. And there are universal truths that can make the task easier.

The first of our maxims is:

Know Yourself

Oscar Wilde once wrote, "I am the only person in the world I should like to know thoroughly." Whether or not you feel that way about yourself, there is much to be gained by a fully rounded understanding of yourself—both as a manager and as a human being.

The plea here is to understand fully both the great gifts with which you have been graced and the inherent shortcomings that accompany those gifts. We must understand those things we do well and the blind spots that often accompany our gifts. When we understand both our gifts and our shortcomings, we can move beyond the shortcomings, leverage the gifts, and motivate ourselves to, in the words of the U.S. Army's long-running recruiting theme: "Be all that we can be." As we do this, it is good to remember that, in the yin and yang of life, all gifts have a shadow side.

The Seeds of Our Destruction Are Sown in Soil Tilled by Our Gifts

The Greek tragedians had it right: however we have been blessed by God or fate, good genes or good fortune, those same gifts can lead to our downfall. We have all seen it a hundred times. In any arena you select, over and over again the drama is played out. In politics, in the religious world, in athletics, and doubtless in the business where you live and work, you have seen people sow the seeds of their destruction in soil tilled with their great gifts.

The persuasive and charming politician time and again squeezes out of sticky situations by the force of his personality. Over and over he does this, and as he does it, he grooves and habituates behavior that will eventually bring about his ruination. He comes to believe that *he is an exception to the rule of accountability*. That he, and only he, can do whatever he pleases and escape consequences. Because he is charming, articulate, and empathetic, people will "let it slide."

And he is right, too, for a while. Time and again he weasels out of tight spots with a smile on his face and a ready quip on his tongue, only to ultimately run into a wall of liability when he pushes the boundaries too far and too often on his journey of irresponsible unaccountability.

How can we avoid this same outcome? The answer is amazingly *simple*, though quite *difficult*.

Know Your Weaknesses: Grow and Staff around Them

We must know our weaknesses and grow and staff around them. That is, we must fully understand the places we are most likely to fail, and surround ourselves with people who will prevent us from failing in those areas. Simultaneously, we must continue to press ourselves to grow, so that our *weak spot eventually becomes a place of competence* and we are less likely to wander into a minefield of self-destruction, following the compass of our gifts.

Staffing around our weaknesses can, however, cause some interpersonal chaffing, because people whose strengths countervail against our weaknesses often *seem* to us to be incompatible.

Nobody Is Sane—You're Looking for Compatible Craziness

Syndicated humor columnist Dave Barry said it this way: "Nobody is normal." However you say it, it's the truth. We're not looking for sanity, perfection, or normalcy. *We're looking for compatible craziness.*

As you staff around your weaknesses, seek people with corresponding strengths, people with whom you can work as collegial partners. Their personal compatibility with you is equally as important as their professional competence. (It's a rare person among us who can work continuously with someone we intensely dislike—irrespective of how well he does his job!)

So look for compatible craziness. Staff around your weaknesses, but don't abrogate your obligation to develop areas in which you are weak.

Take Yourself On

Take yourself on. Reflect on your life. How are you likely to fail those around you? What do you do especially well?

In what circumstances do you do your best work? What motivates you?

Observe yourself as you move through life to see what patterns you can discern and what lessons you can learn. Do you procrastinate so badly that your teammates suffer and your work quality plummets? Do something about it! Don't settle for the lame rationalization that "it's just the way I am." It may be the way you were *born*, but it doesn't have to be how you *live*! Buy a time management system or take a course to help you become better. Corner a nonprocrastinating colleague and find out how she finishes projects without a last minute sprint. If none of that works, find a counselor and talk it over. Is it fear that causes your procrastination? What are you afraid of: the project? Success? Failure?

Know yourself so you can take yourself on. It's a life-long task, one at which we will never become perfect. It requires enormous discipline, because we are calling ourselves to go against our natural grain: to become people who have developed the shadow sides of our temperament and our gifts, to become people who are now fully rounded and whole.

This is a journey many people do not have the courage to undertake; one whose rewards far outweigh the costs. It's a journey that requires *action*.

It's Easier to Act Yourself into a New Way of Thinking Than to Think Yourself into a New Way of Acting

This is a foundational precept of cognitive therapy: the belief that if we begin to *act in a certain way, the actions will lead (and form) our thinking*. If you *act* like a confident, engaging speaker, you will eventually (with preparation and hard work) *think* like a confident, engaging speaker. And that, in turn, will lead you to *become* a confident, engaging speaker.

So, as you face challenges that threaten to overwhelm you, a first step is to act. *Act* like someone who can solve the problem (even if you don't *think* that someone is you).

We cautioned earlier about confusing motion with progress, and it's a caution to remember. Conversely, no progress is possible without motion. It's impossible, for example, to change the direction of any large object (a ship, an airplane, an automobile) without motion that moves the object forward. Only in the moving forward can corrective forces (rudders, steering gear) make incremental adjustments that bring the object to the more-desirable course.

So, as you manage yourself, cultivate a predisposition to positive, on-purpose action. It will make all of life much easier.

Be Your Own Best Boss

Our ultimate charge is to *be our own best boss*. To incorporate—in our self-management as well as our other-management—all that we know to be true about good management. Here's an illustrative story from my own foray into the world of self-management.

I once had to slog my way through a difficult and seemingly interminable project. I got through it only by "being my own best boss," by setting intermediate milestones for myself and rewarding myself when I achieved those milestones.

Thus, as I polished the proposal for the project and prepared to submit it, I set a drop-dead due date and a reward for reaching that date. I picked a time forty-five days in the future as a due date, and promised myself I would have the final proposal in the mail by that date. I then assured myself that if I reached that goal, I could reward myself with a professional massage. With that carrot hanging in front of me, I finished the proposal, made the submission deadline, and enjoyed a "much-kneaded" hour and a half.

In this instance, I motivated myself in the same way we advocate motivating employees in Chapter 2. I picked a reward equal to the effort required by the project (Question 4,

Figure 2-2), and this payoff motivated me to get the project done on time. So, I was my own best boss.

Beyond selecting the right reward, however, I was my own best boss in other ways. I painted myself a SMART target. The project was challenging, but not impossible. I set a specific due date, and I rewarded progress and outcomes, not motion or activities. Finally, I paid off in currency that mattered to me.

It is in the area of motivation that good self-management can have the greatest impact. Chapter 2 taught us that we can never motivate other people, and that is true. We can, however, create an environment in which other people motivate themselves—even when the "other person" is us.

We *read the results* of others' efforts *in actions* and *not in intentions*. This statement is also true for self-management. We cannot "read" the effects of our attempts to motivate ourselves except in productive outcomes achieved. And we are most likely to achieve those productive outcomes when we have created an environment in which we can motivate ourselves. That is, when we create an environment in which our payoffs for on-target and purposeful behavior are clear and appropriate, and our consequences for off-target and off-purpose behavior are severe enough to avoid. Shaping appropriate motivators is critical work, because the world seems to hold only two kinds of workers.

There Are Two Types of People: Them That Won't Work, and Them That Won't Quit 👍

I once heard a Presbyterian preacher comment that: "Only two types of people enter the ministry—them that won't work, and them that won't quit." There's a kernel of truth here that informs the challenge we face when we begin to evaluate our own activities. It's often *difficult to determine how hard we are working.* And we are sometimes more forgiving of sloth in our own activities than in the activities of those we supervise. I was reflecting on my tendency to let up on myself—to give in to fatigue or exhaustion—when a colleague gave me an insight that has helped me press on to finish hard tasks.

You Always Pass Out before You Die! 👍

This maxim reminds me of a poster from the free-weight room in a fitness center I once attended. It would make a great companion to its partner: "Sweat is what happens when muscles cry!"

I don't know if it is a physiological truth that we always pass out before we die. I have never pushed myself—intellectually or physically—to the point of a coma. But I do know that it is an aphorism that has sustained me when I was fatigued and trying to slog through the last difficult steps of a project. You always pass out before you die—so if I'm still conscious, I keep working.

As you keep working, you will undoubtedly encounter situations that aren't going the way you planned. You will meet problems that must be solved, difficult and vexing circumstances that must be faced and dealt with. Here are some maxims I have found useful in these circumstances—maxims that helped me stay focused on finding solutions rather than pointing fingers or getting "hooked" emotionally.

Problems Live in the Past; Solutions Live in the Future

Problems live in the past. It is often easy, as we journey into the land of problem solving and conflict resolution, to get so wrapped up in talking about the problem that we never look to the future for the solution. This is a mistake.

None of us is fortunate enough to have a rewind button on life. We can't simply reach up and press that button, undo the wrong and make it right. The wrong has been *done*.

Our only option is to make changes so that the wrong is not repeated. So we look to the past only long enough to identify root causes for the problems we encounter. Then we become future-focused, realizing that the solution to the problem lies in the future, the only place we yet have a chance to go, live, and act.

Be Solutions-Focused: Concentrate on Win-Win Outcomes

For some reason, problems pull out the petulant four-year-old in each of us. A problem occurs, and our first inclination is to point a finger. We must lay the blame, bring the charges, and hold the trial. Then we find someone guilty and level a sentence. Everyone (except the victim of the system) feels better. And the problem just sits there, unsolved and smirking.

As we move toward managing ourselves professionally, we need to let go of this model. We want a solution, not a trial. So we embrace the wisdom of Robert Smith from Chapter 5: "I'm not here to prosecute the guilty; I'm here to solve the problem."

We visit the problem long enough to uncover key facts. We probe possible solutions, looking for overlapping areas of interest. We find the solution that will do the most good for the most people, then we put that solution in place.

The Madder You Get, the Dumber You Are

I never met a person who could make better decisions when angry than when calm. We even have a word for this: irrational. Not rational. Not thinking.

Who among us has not—in the heat of an argument—said and done things that we would have moved heaven and earth to unsay and undo when we finally returned to our rational state. Our observations and our lived experience validate it: the madder we get, the dumber we are.

Our challenge, then, is to manage ourselves in a way that we can avoid anger—at least the trembling anger that leaves us sputtering rather than speaking. Anger creates situations that rupture relationships, ruptured relationships lead to enemies, and enemies accumulate.

Friends Come and Friends Go, but Enemies Accumulate

It's a sad fact of life, to be sure. And it's also true. Friends *do* come and go, especially in a society as mobile as ours. And enemies do accumulate—the list slowly building from accumulated unbalanced investment ledgers, or as the fruit of being madder (and dumber) than appropriate in a given circumstance. And none of us has more friends than we need, or fewer enemies than would benefit us. Self-management—actually anger management—is critical to slow the accumulation of enemies and help us to be effective in our business and professional relationships. (Remember our maxim from Chapter 5: you don't have to be mad to give developmental feedback.)

One factor that contributes to flash-point anger and hair-trigger responses is fatigue: exhaustion born of overwork and under-recreation. It's often bewitching for us to believe we are indispensable, and to consequently dispense with our own vacation so that we can stay at our desk and slog away. Don't do it!

In Twenty Years, the Only Person Who Will Remember That You Didn't Take Your Vacation Is You (and Your Family)!

You've seen 'em, and so have I: the folks who are married to their work. They slave over their desks, never leaving for vacation or much of any other reason. I don't know why they do it; perhaps they have an unarticulated expectation of a grand payoff based on HBD (Hours Behind the Desk). Don't be one of these!

An organization is not a living entity: it does not have a memory. Your family, on the other hand, does have a memory. They will remember the vacations forgone so that you could stay at work and "finish this last report." Each family member will remember the sports events you missed, the family holidays you could not attend, and all the myriad ways they were shortchanged by your devotion to business. And it will not be worth it.

As you have doubtless heard, few people remark on their deathbeds, "I sure wish I'd spent more time at work." So take that vacation. Leave that cell phone and laptop at home, and re-create with your family and yourself that sense of joy and peace that comes from leisure time well spent.

Time away from the job refreshes your mind. You come back to work with a new perspective, you have the energy to tackle a project that once seemed dreadful, and you have the patience to deal with a frustrating employee. While time away is profoundly restorative, the return transition can be wrenching. So when you return, always remember our next aphorism.

Never Quit on the First Day Back!

I don't know how many times I have returned from a relaxing vacation, only to get sucked into the vortex of overflowing in-baskets, flashing red lights on my voice mail, and email that scrolled for pages and pages.

Vacations are a paradoxical joy, anyhow. The run-up to the vacation is highly anticipated, accompanied by frantic activity as we try to move all the work from the coming week into the current week, so that we can complete it and feel free to leave.

Consequently, we leave for vacation exhausted, and spend four days recovering from the frantic preparations. We enjoy the final three days of the time away, then return on Monday morning to an office that looks like a mail truck hit a bookmobile and the results of the explosion were dumped on our desks.

At this point I always want to quit. Too many phone messages, too many emails, too many voice mails, too much mail, period. I say to myself, "I hate this job! It wasn't this bad before I left…" You will want to quit, too. Don't. What you are experiencing is the inevitable reentry from the world of leisure and recreation to a world of production and commerce. The latter funds the former, so give them both their due and stay with it long enough to remember why you chose this vocation in the first place.

As we close our reflection on self-management, it's imperative to remind yourself of this last adage.

It's Okay to Fire Yourself

I've certainly been there; I bet you have, too. Dragging along in a job that is less and less satisfying—where you find yourself doing work that embarrasses you more and more. You stay in the job because inertia is a powerful force, and you're comfortable.

This is the point where you should fire yourself. Either fire yourself up with enthusiasm for the job, get off your duff, and start being the professional you once were when you loved the job, or fire yourself from the job. Find a job you like better, and begin to embrace it with the passion you once exhibited for the job you now hold. Either way, it's okay to fire yourself!

Self-management: it's the toughest nut of all, because you are the toughest nut you will ever have to manage. But it's imperative if you are to become the manager you want to be and take your company to the places that it needs to go.

✦ MAXIMS ON ✦ SELF-MANAGEMENT

Know yourself.

The seeds of our destruction are sown in soil tilled by our gifts.

Know your weaknesses: grow and staff around them.

Nobody is sane—you're looking for compatible craziness.

Take yourself on.

It's easier to act your way into a new way of thinking than to think your way into a new way of acting.

Be your own best boss.

There are two types of people: them that won't work, and them that won't quit.

You always pass out before you die.

Problems live in the past; solutions live in the future.

Be solutions-focused: concentrate on win-win outcomes.

The madder you get, the dumber you are.

Friends come and friends go; enemies accumulate.

In twenty years, the only person who will remember you didn't take your vacation is you (and your family)!

Never quit on the first day back.

It's okay to fire yourself.

QUESTIONS FOR REFLECTION

1. What seeds of destruction have been sown in soil tilled by your gifts? How can you mitigate against the shadow side of your gifts?

2. What do you consider your greatest weaknesses? How can you grow and staff around them?

3. There are two kinds of people: them that won't work, and them that won't quit. Which are you? How does this work style affect your ability to relate to your followers?

4. Have you ever fired yourself? Why did you do it? How did it work out?

CHALLENGE FOR APPLICATION

Think about how you enter into problems and conflicts. What can you do to remain solutions-focused? How can you get to a win-win outcome more often, with less pain and suffering?

9

LEADERSHIP

eadership—like motivation—is quicksilver and ephemeral. It's hard to define precisely but easy to recognize when you encounter it. Like motivation, leadership has been plagued with a myriad of theories, dictates, models, and often-conflicting directives. Leadership is a critical and difficult topic—one that has fascinated human beings for centuries.

Whatever your theory, there are some things about leadership that are fundamentally true. This chapter is devoted to those truths.

Any Follower's Experience of a Group Is Most Directly Affected by the Leadership Style of the Leader

Reflect on your own experiences in organizations—both pleasant and unpleasant. Remember the athletic team on which you played? The one for which you would get out of a sickbed to go to practice because the esprit de corps among your team members was so vibrant? Doubtless, this had much to do with the leadership style of your leader—the coach.

Perhaps it was an experience in your church choir—a choir where you felt valued and an important part of the team. You felt like you were learning and contributing simultaneously, and were eager to show up—both for rehearsals and services. Your enthusiasm probably derived at least partially from the leadership style of your choir director.

Maybe it was a civic club, a work group of which you were a part, or some other organization—a group that coalesced around a leader who created an environment in which you wanted to be led and in which you valued her leadership.

Clearly, the leadership style at the apex of an organizational pyramid is a critical characteristic in determining the experience of all those who find themselves within the organization. In fact, this is the impetus behind our next maxim.

You Can Best Read the Climate of an Organization by Surveying Those Who Actually *Do* the Work

The people who do the work are the ones closest to the customer and to the end product. They have the best and most unbiased read on the true tenor of the organization. And their experience of the organization is most directly affected by the leadership style of their immediate leader.

Note the word "immediate" in the above sentence. It is possible (in fact, quite likely) that you have observed pockets of happiness and competence inside organizations that were overall a hopeless morass of disenchanted, demotivated petulance. Likewise, even in the most motivated and high-energy organizations, there are always small pockets of discontent and grumbling. The one single thread running through these pockets—pockets that are discontinuous with the overall organization—is the leader. Look at the leader and you can predict what his immediate organization will be like. The single greatest predictor of happiness and productivity in a work group is the level of conscious, intentional, competent *service* provided by the leader.

Those Lead Best Who Serve Most

This is one of the most telling aphorisms in this chapter. It is those leaders whose ultimate goal is to serve—to serve both the followers *and* the greater reason for the organization—who wind up generating esprit de corps, enthusiasm, highly motivated followers, and successful achievement of difficult goals. These leaders' service to their groups can take many forms: crafting a vision; communicating the vision; providing resources for the team members; selecting, training, and getting feedback from team members; advocating for the team with higher authority; interpreting to the followers the edicts and policies of higher authorities; and performing myriad other tasks.

Always, though, the leader is acting in a way that best *serves* the needs of his followers, the organization, and the constituencies the organization is shaped to serve. Examples of this type of leadership are myriad and can be gleaned from all areas of human endeavor. Mahatma Gandhi served the people of India (and ultimately, the rulers of the British Empire as well) by articulating a vision for a new India, and communicating that vision in a nonviolent but profoundly persuasive way to England and the world.

Decades later, Martin Luther King Jr. adopted some of Gandhi's philosophy, brought it into the American racial equality movement, and used it to steer the movement between the rocky shoals of racial schism and the dangerous currents of profound violence. In serving his movement and his country, he led us to a much more peaceable outcome than would have otherwise been achieved. Dr. King did this by serving the needs of black Americans and articulating his vision for a just society to a larger, racist America.

Moving beyond the political arena, the sports world is filled with examples of coaches whose primary function was the service of the people who played for them. Basketball legend Dean Smith of the University of North Carolina was well-known for his ongoing allegiance to those who played for him. He *served* them by keeping their best interests at heart, even if their interests conflicted with those of the university's rabid fans. On more than one occasion, Smith advised players to leave the University of North Carolina for professional careers before they had finished their college tenure. Coach Smith reasoned that no twenty-year-old man should pass up the opportunity to make millions of dollars if that opportunity was right before his eyes.

In the business arena, there are also leaders who serve their followers, although it's a little harder to discern because the teams are so much bigger and the examples less public. A story from the early days of Ford's creation of its wildly successful Taurus automobile bears repeating. When he ascended to the presidency of Ford, Donald Peterson was taken on a tour through the design studios of Ford Motor Company. There he encountered the design team working on the Ford Taurus. The Taurus had not yet been introduced; much was riding on the successful introduction of a new mid-sized vehicle that would appeal to a broad segment of the American public.

Peterson reviewed the proposed designs, the clay models, the mockups, and the sketches. He then turned to the design team and said something to the effect of, "What would this car look like if you were allowed to design it from the ground up the way you thought best—unfettered by organizational constraints?"

This was not a thought that the design team had been allowed to think, nor a question they had been asked. And it generated the enthusiasm and hard work that led to the "jellybean design" of the mid-1980s and ultimately to a year when the Ford Taurus was the largest-selling single model style in the American automobile business. Peterson *served* his followers by giving them the latitude to do their best work, and the results were astounding.

Service can take many forms. Here's a story about the juxtaposition between self-service and true service.

I once played football for a bright, driven, aggressive coach in his late twenties. He was a firebrand, a yeller, and a screamer. Late in our undefeated season, we were blowing out a clearly over-matched opponent. In the second half, I made a mistake and our team lost about fifteen yards.

The coach called time out, and the quarterback jogged to the sideline. He quickly returned, indicating that the coach wanted to see *me*. I trotted over and was met by the most enraged person I'd ever seen. He screamed and ranted, cursed and railed. He humiliated me in front of an entire stadium full of fans, then sent me back on the field.

Why did he do this? I do not know. I suppose the coach was trying to motivate me, but all he did was motivate me to never play another season for him. And that's often the fruit of self-serving actions; actions (like his blowup) that assuage the leader but do nothing to connect with the followers.

And now a story about *true* service. In graduate business school, I had another bright, aggressive, and driven coach. He was a professor, and he was *good*.

Once he assigned us a case, and I did a good—but not great—job on it. I got it back and received a B. Not bad, I thought. Then I read a classmate's case; this guy had gotten an A. But, in my (unbiased, no doubt) opinion, his work was inferior to mine.

So I went to the professor. I laid out my observations. I pointed out the holes in my classmate's work, and the strengths of mine. And I queried: "What's the deal?" He leaned way back in his chair, looked me dead in the eye, and said, "I try to give people the grade that will do 'em the most good."

"What?" I sputtered.

"I try to give people the grade that will do 'em the most good. You're right—your case is better than your classmate's. But you're not competing with him. You're competing with yourself. Your classmate gave me his best work. So he gets an A. You gave me good work, but not your best. So you get a B. I wanted you to know that I can tell the difference. Give me *your* best, and *you'll* get an A, too!"

I never again goofed off in that class. My professor *served me well* when he tailored his response to my specific needs, abilities, and shortcomings. I knew he knew the difference, and he pulled superior performance from me in every subsequent case and class.

It's hard work to respond to our followers individually. It's also the best way to serve them.

So, those lead best who serve most. As we reflect on our many roles in our organization—and the conflicting priorities that are forever clamoring for our attention—we must remember to make those decisions that best serve the long-term interests of our people, our organization, our customers, and the other constituencies to which we are accountable.

Remarkably, *once we begin to serve, leadership will take care of itself.* The best major religious leaders of the last three millennia have all been servants. An enduring legacy of service is one of the best things we can leave as a memorial to ourselves—far beyond financial empires, granite monuments, or the florid praise that accompanies the obituaries of the currently famous and newly dead. So service is a foundational precept for leadership. It is one key; there are others. Another fundamental requirement of good leaders is that they remember to *do* what they already *know* how to do.

> # It's Not What We Don't *Know* That Gets Us in Trouble—It's What We Don't *Do*

Think for a moment about the thousands of traffic accidents that will occur in America today, the dozens of people who will die on our highways. Is the problem that these people do not *know* they should not run red lights, pass over the double yellow line, or drive while drinking alcoholic beverages? No! That is *not* the problem. The problem is that people are *not doing what they already know* how to do. They are not bringing into their everyday behavior the head knowledge they have about how to drive safely.

So, too, it can be with leadership. We know that *input raises buy-in*. We have heard it, we have observed it, we believe it to be true. Yet we repeatedly fall back into our old patterns of making decisions by executive fiat and imposing them on our followers. Then we are surprised when our followers do not embrace these decisions with open arms and give us accolades for being such visionary decision-makers.

Followers like input into decisions—*any* decisions they will have to implement. The more input they have, the more likely they are to embrace the decision that has been made, and to move out with full commitment to ensure that it works. We *serve* our followers by involving them in the decisions where they have a reasonable chance of giving productive input, and by incorporating their suggestions into the direction we take.

However, when the followers have little chance of providing productive input, our obligation is to interpret for them the "why" of the decision. Followers like to know why. We've said it before, and we even *believe* it. But—pressed into a corner and harried for time—we issue directives about the "what" of our organization without ever treating the "why." And we wonder about the dispirited atmosphere in our workplaces and the high turnover rates we have among key employees.

When we move out into our organization to allow people to have input and when we articulate the "why" of corporate policies, we are filling two key roles. Our job as leaders is to *interpret* "down" and *advocate* "up." Let's reflect on these concepts in a little more detail.

As a Manager, You Are a "Linking Pin"—You Link Your Work Group to the Larger Company

I once heard a mentor of mine say that managers and leaders are "linking pins," *linking* their work group to an organization. I grew up in an agricultural environment, so I knew exactly what he was talking about. A linking pin is a stout metal pin that, when dropped through a small hole in the back of a tractor drawbar, links a tobacco wagon or some other farm implement to the tractor. Likewise, managers are linking pins who connect their work group or department to the overall organization. And effective work as a linking pin demands that we serve two roles.

We *interpret* the policies of the larger organization to those who are our followers. That is, we tell them the "why." Why is it that our company has decided to change our product line? Or raise our prices? Or not pursue particular markets? These are questions our followers want to know the answers to, questions that will plague them and raise doubts in their minds if they are not addressed fully. So one of our roles is to fully articulate and interpret the "why" of corporate decisions.

This is harder than it seems. Inevitably, corporate management will make decisions with which we do not agree.

The temptation is always to move out into our team and make a comment that begins: "Those morons at corporate have decided…." It's an enticing option, but a poor choice. This technique—called "transparent management" by some management theorists—removes us as a member of the management team and makes us "one of the guys." And for the near term, that's fun.

Eventually, however, management will make a decision with which we fully agree. And we will stand before our team to articulate the decision and encourage them to embrace it. We will tell them what a great idea this decision is, and why they should embrace it and move forward with full enthusiasm to accomplish the goals embodied in the decision. They will then look at us and say, "But I thought you said management was a bunch of morons!" In practicing transparent management, we abdicated our role as interpreters and lost our influence over our group. Further, we are not *serving* them by fully helping them understand the implications for—and reasons behind—a particular corporate decision.

Interpretation, however, is not enough. Our second role as leaders is to *advocate* for our followers. And we advocate for them by gathering their concerns and understanding their needs, then articulating those needs to the organizational hierarchy above us. Put differently, we solicit their input and advocate that input upward to heighten the work group's buy-in to the corporate goal.

MANAGER AS LINKING PIN

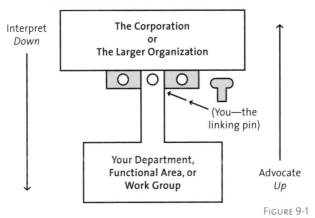

Interpret
Down

The Corporation
or
The Larger Organization

(You—the
linking pin)

Your Department,
Functional Area, or
Work Group

Advocate
Up

FIGURE 9-1

These two difficult roles are presented in Figure 9-1: interpreter and advocate. They are both critical if we are to lead those on our teams by serving them in the most helpful way. As leaders we embrace these two roles for several reasons. First, they make *organizational* sense. Interpretation and advocacy are two tasks we must take on if information is to pass up and down our organizational hierarchy efficiently and effectively. Beyond that, however, these dual roles of interpreter and advocate make *relational* sense, too, as evidenced by our next maxim—one of the great truths of human relations.

People Don't Care How Much We Know Until They Know How Much We Care

One way to demonstrate that you care is to let your followers fully into an understanding of why things are being done (*interpret down*). We also demonstrate we care when we advocate for them concerning issues, changes, or ideas about how things can be done better or more productively (*advocate up*).

We demonstrate how much we care by taking seriously our employees' need to know and their need to have input into the decisions, choices, and strategies embraced by our organization. We demonstrate to our teammates how much we care by engaging them as significant and meaningful contributors to the "why" as well as the "what" of our organization's goals. In doing all of this, we are modeling for them the behaviors we want them to display as *they* engage the team members who work directly for them.

I once was lamenting the scarcity of effective, engaged, empathetic, visionary leaders in an organization I managed. As I continued with my pathetic whining, one of my close friends outside the organization said, "You know, Frank, it takes one to know one. It takes one to show one. It takes one to grow one."

He was (albeit a little less gently than I would have preferred) giving me a nudge toward modeling the behaviors I most desperately sought from my followers. My friend helped me understand that if what I wanted was empathetic, concerned, consistent, visionary leaders, then I needed to model the role of an empathetic, concerned, visionary leader. Because, as he said, it took one to know one, to show one, to grow one.

I found, as I began to model the behaviors I sought, that I was soon observing them more frequently in my followers. People being who they are, they will imitate the behaviors they find helpful, useful, and worthy of emulation. As I became better, my people became better. *People don't care how much we know until they know how much we care*, and we demonstrate our caring and concern in our dual roles of interpreter and advocate. Beyond that, as we demonstrate our concern by interpretation and advocacy, we engender interpretation and advocacy from our followers when they interact with their teams. It takes one to know one, to show one, and to grow one. And—as we model this type of leadership—our followers will adopt it and model it for their employees and teammates.

Two additional aphorisms augment the learning proffered by "People don't care how much we know until they know how much we care." They deserve more detailed treatment here.

Managers Don't Win If Their Employees Lose!

This learning comes late to many managers. They assume that they exist above and apart from their teams, and that they can impose on or communicate to their teams policies that cause the team to lose while the manager is winning. These are leaders and managers who are unfamiliar with the basic plot line of *Mutiny on the Bounty*. Long-term, managers do not win if their employees lose.

This recalls an earlier statement that "Those lead best who serve most." We must serve our followers by making sure that they receive outcomes, rewards, and affirmations that feel like "winning." And if it's not possible for us to yield them a "win," we must be absolutely certain that they know that we are all in this together. We must communicate that—if the team has lost, the manager has lost as well, and is together with the team in a common loss. It does a manager, a team leader, or a coach no good to win at the expense of his team. Teams have long memories, and small gains accrued at the expense of the team will yield huge long-term deficits to the leader. Managers don't win if their employees lose.

What Do You Want to Do: Win the Fight or Solve the Problem?

In line with our assertion that managers don't win if employees lose is a second insight I gleaned from one of my great mentors. Lee Kleese had been a colonel in the United States Army—a hell-for-leather, pedal-to-the-metal, kick-ass leader of the type I would have followed anywhere.

I did not meet Kleese in a military context. He came into my organization as a consultant when I worked as a senior manager in a medium-size private business. This was a time of great learning for me, since I had a job that was far larger than my experience, and I was being stretched every day as I strove to help this organization reach its aggressive business-growth objectives. Colonel Kleese helped put a new face for me on the assertion that managers don't win if employees lose, and he framed it for me in a way that captured additional wisdom.

One of my great frustrations in this job was working with employees who did not share my sense of commitment to our goals or the vision I had for what the company could become. In my consultations with Kleese, I would rail against these people, frustrated at their inability to grab hold of the vision and move forward in an aggressive way to help us reach our goals. I was always amazed at Kleese's measured responses.

After one particularly vitriolic tirade from me, Kleese leaned back in a chair in my office, stared up toward a corner of the ceiling, and said, "Well, Frank, you've just got to decide. What do you want to do—win the fight, or solve the problem?"

"Whaddya mean?" I sputtered. "I want this turkey to get up off his butt and get on the stick! I want to tell him he can get on-board this train or get off this train, but the train is leaving the station and he needs to decide now! We've got work to do!"

Kleese looked at me with a twinkle in his eye and said, "OK. Then go win the fight. You've got the organizational power to do it. You're his direct manager, go kick his butt. It'll be fun. Call me and I'll come back when you decide you want to solve the problem."

"But…" I sputtered. "This guy sittin' on his behind is a barrier to everybody else. Plus, he's infected the entire organization with his indifferent attitude and failure to be committed to our overarching objectives!"

"I see," said the Colonel. "Looks to me like you want to win the fight. Have fun. Scream at the guy. Come back when you want to solve the problem." The interchange continued for some while, and when it was over, I had had one of those rare "Aha!" experiences that are truly graced moments in life.

In our discussions, Kleese helped me understand that my two goals were mutually exclusive. If I went out and torched the shorts of the employee with whom I was frustrated, I would have fun in the near term. It would be a cathartic experience, and I would feel purged after I ranted and raved. But after the immediate relief, there would then be *two* problems: the *initial* problem that generated my outrage in the first place, and a *second* (more grievous) problem of an employee who felt attacked and demeaned by a superior. There would be two issues to deal with, and in winning the fight I would have exacerbated the problem. And managers don't win when employees lose.

The key for managers in dealing with problem employees and problem situations is to ask ourselves—before we enter the fray—"What particular outcomes will lead us closest to the successful resolution of the problem?" Generally, one of those outcomes is not winning the fight. So the proper stance for us (and, in fact, the stance that is most congruent with our goal to *lead best by serving most*) is to enter every interaction with an employee focused solely on solving the problem.

We are in problem-resolution mode when we look to the future and decide which course of action will most likely take us to a successful solution, and when we give up our need to publicly humiliate or otherwise demean the employee who has created the problem. This is a tremendous phase-shift for any manager. It marks the move from a parental blaming/ shaming management style to an adult management style that is focused more on outcomes than on shame. And more likely to engender loyalty than guilt. It is a critical move for anyone who wants to become a truly professional manager.

The choice is ours: solve the problem and move forward as professional managers ready to take on the next challenge that our organization deals us, or win the fight and stay stuck in the current problem, having exacerbated it by aggravating the employee, and also by unnecessarily using up productive energy that could have gone against the resolution of the core problem.

Interestingly, the win-the-fight/solve-the-problem dilemma dovetails nicely with our next maxim.

Make Your Leadership Style a Choice, Not a Default

For good or ill, most of us, at least as we begin, manage as we were managed by our first manager. Either that, or we manage as we were parented. For many of us, these are not good models.

I'm thinking back to a manager I worked with early in my career. His basic philosophy was Theory X: "People are no damn good, and you have to watch 'em like a hawk."

I once asked him why he did not give any reinforcement or encouragement to the people with whom he worked. His response was, "I ain't thanking that yahoo to do a job I'm paying him to do!" As the sentence left his mouth, I had an immediate image of what it was like for this man as he was growing up in his family. Had his life been a bumper sticker, I suspect it would have been: "Perfection is the minimum acceptable standard!" Coming from a family like this, he managed as he *was* managed. He managed by default, using the style with which he was most familiar.

As people who have been charged by an organization with the obligation of shepherding a business team to reach overarching business goals, *we can't afford to lead by default.* We lead best by serving most when we *know multiple management and leadership styles, and can adopt the one best suited to the group* we now have before us. That's our obligation.

Beyond choosing an appropriate leadership style, we must be consistent. That is, our employees must be able to predict dependably how we will behave in any set of circumstances; we cannot afford to confuse them.

You Can Be a Hardass or You Can Be a Candyass, but You've Got to Be *Consistent*!

I once had an employee tell me, "I can tell what kind of day I'm going to have by watching you shut the door of your car in the parking lot." This is a not a good thing. If the kind of day the employee has is driven by the mood I'm in, I'm doing my team a disservice.

There are enough unpredictable elements in the business world without managers becoming one of them. And as the leader of a team, your obligation to the team is to be a constant in a world of uncertainty. Not only must we make our leadership style a choice, not a default, we must lead out of that style on a consistent basis. Or, as my friend Lee Kleese told me years ago, "You can be a hardass, or you can be a candyass, but you've got to be consistent!"

It's a lesson I've not yet forgotten; I hope I take it to the grave. It was not my employee's job to make me have a good day or to work me out of my moods. It was *my job to suspend my moods* in interactions with my employees so that I was a predictable constant in an unpredictable and transitory world.

When Stressed, We Return to Our Most Familiar—and Most Comfortable—Behaviors

The difficult thing about the assignment to be predictable and constant is that—when stressed—all people return to their most comfortable behaviors. So, absent strong self-control, I will again revert to someone who slams employees around like I slam car doors on bad days.

And that earlier manager—the one who said, "I ain't thanking the yahoo to do a job I'm paying him to do"—will fall back on a gruff, non-affirming style of management that leaves employees wondering about management's receptivity to their good, hard, and purposeful work.

This is not as it should be. We lead best and we serve most by insulating our employees from the vicissitudes of our personal emotional ups and downs. We lead best and serve most when we deal with our followers as professionals, when we act like managers who value employees, and when we lead employees with a purposeful and intentional style that pulls the best performance out of them.

We close out our examination of the key maxims that inform professional leadership with four conceptual maxims that can overarch and undergird our work as leaders. I often have managers come to me and say, "I don't have time to manage my people. I've got too much work to do!" I always chuckle when I hear this—it's as if *doing work* and *managing people* were two separate tasks. And that is not the case at all.

Managing People *Is* Work!

Managing people *is* work. It's a hard transition for many of us to make, especially those of us who were first paid in our working lives for the output we generated from our own hands, minds, and computer terminals and who are now called upon to generate consistently superior performance from other people's work. It is, however, a critical transition.

The next time you think you have too much work to manage your people, ask yourself: what is my *real* work? Realize that managing people *is* work. It takes time, but done well, it will yield far more productive outcomes than you could ever generate alone. Now for our second over-arching aphorism.

Where You Stand Depends on Where You Sit

It has become common in American academic circles for writers to identify their "social location" as they introduce new academic theories and treatises. Social location is nothing more than the writer letting the reader know from whence he comes (educational background, gender, race, sexual orientation, political inclination, family of formation, and academic training). It has become normative in academic circles because it helps the reader understand the viewpoint from which the writer has written. And it is equally important in professional managerial circles as it is in academic circles. Hence our aphorism: where you stand depends on where you sit.

One of our jobs as we make decisions, as we advocate for our people, as we interpret policies from the upper organization to our immediate direct reports, is to be conscious of the position in which we stand so that we will be fully aware of where we sit on an issue. As middle managers making decent salaries and living comfortably, we may not be markedly affected by a small increase in the deductibles in a health insurance policy. We probably have the money to underwrite that increase. That, however, may not be the case for our lower-paid employees with large families who will be directly hit in the pocketbook by this benefits change.

We need to understand that where they stand on the issue depends on where they sit—which is in a home with limited resources and multiple demands on those resources. Being able to get inside our own and our employees' minds will yield dramatic insights (and results) on issues like this. It will also be a way of *informing our advocacy* as we talk to our managers (and their managers) about the impact of changes on our employees.

It's critical in situations like this to remember that our employees don't care how much we know until they know how much we care. One way we demonstrate caring in a situation like this is by understanding the position from which the other comes; that is, by understanding that where they stand depends on the position in which they sit.

Two final key learnings for managers: many management trainers and theorists spend a great deal of time teaching their followers and their disciples how to "control" interactions and situations with employees. This seems to me to be an inordinate waste of time. Who cares who's in control? Who cares who makes the decision? The important thing is the ultimate outcome.

I Don't Care Who Drives as Long as I Get to Pick the Destination

There's no need to get wrapped around the axle about who's controlling the interaction, especially if the interaction is moving logically toward an outcome that the manager seeks in the first place. If we believe (and I do) that input raises buy-in, why short-circuit an employee's authentic attempt to have input into the decision by "controlling" the interaction? If the employee is going where you want him to go, provide him with resources and get the hell out of the way!

Finally, it's important for each of us as leaders to remember that—though we have to get it all done—we don't have to *do* it all.

The Leader Doesn't Have to Do It All. The Leader Has to See That It All Gets Done!

We were all first promoted for our facility at *doing* a task. Now our task is to *pull superior performance out of those who work for us.* The sooner we realize that managing people *is* work, and the sooner we free ourselves to *lead rather than merely to do,* the better job we will do for our employees, our organization, ourselves, and all the other constituencies we serve.

⚔ MAXIMS ON LEADERSHIP ⚔

Any follower's experience of a group is most directly affected by the leadership style of the leader.

You can best read the climate of an organization by surveying those who actually do the work.

Those lead best who serve most.

It's not what we don't *know* that gets us in trouble—it's what we don't *do*.

As a manager, you are a "linking pin"—you link your work group to the larger company.

People don't care how much we know until they know how much we care.

Managers don't win if their employees lose.

What do you want to do: win the fight or solve the problem?

Make your leadership style a choice, not a default.

You can be a hardass or you can be a candyass, but you've got to be *consistent*.

When stressed, we return to our most familiar—and most comfortable—behaviors.

Managing people *is* work.

Where you stand depends on where you sit.

I don't care who drives as long as I get to pick the destination.

The leader doesn't have to do it all. The leader has to see that it all gets done.

QUESTIONS FOR REFLECTION

1. Do you believe those who lead best are those who serve most? Why or why not? How can you better serve your followers?

2. As a linking pin in your organization, which do you do better: interpret or advocate? How could you develop your weaker skill set (interpretation or advocacy) to make yourself a better leader?

3. What do you do to demonstrate to your followers that you care? How does it work? How do you know?

4. What is your preferred leadership style? Did you choose it, or muddle into it? How could you tweak it to be more effective?

CHALLENGE FOR APPLICATION

Think about a current leadership role you have. How are you leading in this situation? Is it effective? How could you serve these followers more effectively? What about your leadership style needs to change so that you can do a better job for this team?

10

SHAPING YOUR MANAGEMENT PHILOSOPHY

What's your management philosophy? This is not the kind of question we spend much time reflecting upon. Our time is consumed with labor-rate variances, market share accretions, and people problems.

Our philosophy of management often springs from either how we were managed at home or from the formative managers we had in the business world. *We learn what we live*, so these experiences imprint upon us in a powerful way.

Significantly, we also learn other lessons that markedly influence our management philosophy. We (most of us, anyhow) learn to be nice, to please others, and to avoid conflict. And these lessons can block our effectiveness as managers. We are so busy trying to be *pleasant*, that we abrogate our obligation to be *professional*. Whatever your ultimate management philosophy, you might find this first maxim to be quite liberating.

A Hundred Percent of Nobody Don't Like Nothing

No doubt, some long-ago English teacher cautioned you against using double negatives. Intoned—interminably, perhaps—that "a double negative equals a positive." I don't know. I wasn't good at math *or* English.

What I *do* know is this: you can't make 'em all happy. So don't try. Don't ground your management philosophy in the most-recent plebiscite conducted among your peers and followers. If you do, you will have your work group lurching wildly about like a sailboat without a rudder. You'll be tossed in a tempest of ever-changing whim, on a sea of management fads and fallacies. You'll be yanked first this way and then the other—influenced by storms of temperamental pique that'll push your boat off-course and threaten to wreck it on the shoals of uncertainty and indecision.

I'm not sure what the key to success is, but the key to failure is trying to please everyone else. So give it up. Make the best decision you have with the data before you. Survey the resources at your disposal; weigh the options. Then choose. Choose, go forward, and don't look back. Because a hundred percent of nobody don't like nothing.

No Matter What Happens, Somebody Will Find a Way to Take It Far Too Seriously

How true, how true. Have you ever noticed that—no matter what happens—it hits someone's hot button?

A friend of mine is a minister, and this is her continual lament. Change the order of service? Some love it; some hate it. Fix it back as it was and the groups reverse. Add a nine o'clock service? One group is excited and embraces it. Another rails against it.

Why is this true? Who knows? *Is it true?* Absolutely!

Don't misunderstand me here—work is important. It's how we make the money that puts food on the table and a roof over our heads. Work stores value for future retirement, and allows us to use our gifts in the service of others. For some people, work even gives meaning to life.

But work is *not* life. And it's important to remember this, both in times of great jubilation (when we feel ten feet tall and bulletproof) and in times of great despair (when we're hip-deep in muck and sinking fast!). No matter what happens, someone will find a way to take it too seriously. Don't let that someone be *you*.

Find ways and means outside of work to enrich and deepen

your core self—who you really are. Stay grounded in some reality greater than your last quarterly earnings report or your most recent annual review. It is only the things of transcendent value that can sustain us when work goes to hell.

Our first two maxims dealt with overarching observations that can help us shape our management philosophy. We now move to more pointed aphorisms—those that can inform how we interact with the people in our organization.

It's Okay to Ask 'Em to Work

There are a lot of things we must do to be good managers. We must shape a vision for the organization we lead, and articulate that vision to our followers. We must paint SMART targets for our followers, and create environments in which they can motivate themselves.

We must teach and coach, measure performance and payoff in currency that matters to our employees. We must manage ourselves, and we must audit our relationships to make sure they are equitable and in balance. All of these are key pieces to the managerial puzzle.

But sooner or later—*you've got to ask'em to work.*

That's the deal. That's how the employee keeps his relationship with us in balance. We provide clear goals, good coaching, and honest feedback. We shape rewards and consequences that match the employee's motivational profile. We provide tools and raw materials and a place to do the work. Sooner or later, the employee has to *work*. And it's our job to ask 'em.

Much of American business seems to have lost sight of this truth. And I'm not sure how that happened.

Perhaps it was the inevitable overcorrection from a period of demanding management patterned after a dictatorial military model. As the pendulum reached its apex and swung back, it gathered speed and whizzed right by a balanced midpoint to the other pole. A place where managers are *afraid* to ask employees to work.

No matter the source, the situation exists. Managers are *afraid* to ask their people to work. And that's a big problem.

It's okay to ask 'em to work. In fact, it's *imperative* to ask 'em to work. Paint a clear picture of a SMART target. Coach well, with specific, targeted, positive, and developmental feedback. Shape rewards and consequences that matter to the employee before you. Then *ask 'em to do the work*!

This is not arrogant. This is not bossy. This is not pushy or impolite or dictatorial. *This is your job!* And you must do it directly and openly—unencumbered by ambiguity. You must ask your employee to do the job. Then ask him if he is going to do it—*get a commitment*.

Get a Commitment

When you ask someone to do a job, you've taken the first—but not the only—step you need to take. A most important step remains: get a commitment. Get the employee's commitment to complete the project, to the specifications, within the budget, by the time agreed upon.

Of course you use input to get buy-in, as we discussed in Chapter 1. Surely you use all the skills we've talked about in our work together. And in the end, you *get that commitment*. You ask: "Are you committed to do this as we've discussed? Do I have your commitment to complete this project by the due date?" Any time you give someone a project, you're selling. So don't forget to ask for the order!

You Can Help the People Change, or You Can Change the People

Managers have substantial and serious obligations to the teams they have been dealt. It's our job to coach them and teach them—to help them grow and be all they can be. It's our job to take seriously their concerns and advocate upward. And it's our job to interpret for them all the various "whys" for corporate and organizational decisions.

It is also our job to help them change, when change is what is called for. We help them learn new skills and we help them develop strengths where they once had weaknesses. We help them grow—because it's our job.

But it's not our job to care more than they care. Some people won't change—whether it's learning a new skill or correcting a problem behavior. I don't know why. I'm not a shrink.

But I do know this: it's not your job to care more than they care. If you have asked 'em to change and provided tools, shaped appropriate rewards and consequences, painted SMART targets and given on-target feedback, you've done your part.

Help your people change, or change your people. That's how I'm asking *you* to work, because it's your job.

Don't Send Your Ducks to Eagle School

As we ask our employees to change, we must bump the requested change up against the employees' skill set and knowledge set. There's no use asking people to do things at which they will inevitably fail.

Take the maxim literally for a moment. Neither ducks nor eagles could do the other's job well. Duck-ness requires amphibian skills—ducks swim, dive, waddle, and fly. They nest in low-lying areas near water, and eat a seafood diet. Eagle-ness, on the other hand, is an entirely different program. Eagles nest in high and inaccessible places. They catch updrafts and soar for hours. They can't swim a lick. But eagles don't need to swim.

Each of these birds is uniquely gifted for their respective calling and would fail in the other's calling. So it can be for our employees. We serve our employees by helping them identify their gifts, and then matching them with jobs that best suit those gifts. This requires that we know them— know their strengths and their weaknesses, their aspirations and their dreams. It also requires that we suspend favoritism and prejudice when we assign employees tasks.

Early in my work life, I observed a manager sending ducks to eagle school. Four people were assigned to a new task. The manager used the "favorites" model for selecting the people. The task was to become in-house trainers for a sales management course. And in many ways, this manager sent ducks to eagle school.

Remember, the task was *training*. The effective-trainer class cost thousands of dollars and took the nominees out of their regular jobs for a week. These employees were to be responsible for training the next generation of salespeople in this company.

One of the nominees—clearly the favorite of the favorites—was a dictatorial, controlling, insecure middle manager. He dealt with his insecurity by being an "expert" and would not listen to others. He ignored the whole training, was an abysmal failure himself, and was fired in less than two years for gross dereliction of duties.

A second nominee—another favorite of the favorites—quit the company four months after the sessions and took his new-found knowledge to a major competitor. He was more a snake than a duck!

The third employee was nice and affable. He didn't make waves, and that's why he was selected. He learned the material and could present it in a workmanlike fashion. He probably did the best of the lot.

The fourth employee was likely the best trainer of the bunch, but he was mercurial and temperamental and was ultimately fired after repeated clashes with the company's owners. He may have been an eagle, but he couldn't exist in this aviary!

So the moral of the story is: don't send your ducks to eagle school. Good ducks make bad eagles. Let your employees be who (and what) they are. But demand that they be the best that they can be.

> # Once You Demand Excellence, Some People Will Move Up and Others Will Move On—Either Way, the Organization Wins

The demand for excellence will have two disparate effects on your employees. Some will be energized. Others will be afraid. It's your job to maximize the first group and minimize the second.

A scenario: you take over a work group that has been struggling. Their productivity is below company norms in both quantity and quality. Several good people have posted-out of the department, and two of the best ones recently quit the company altogether. You come in, articulate a clear vision of excellence, and begin to move the team forward. What's going to happen?

Remember, *the folks remaining in the work group could stand it the way it was.* The more motivated members of the group (see Chapter 2) have already dealt with their problems—they hit the road. So how will those remaining react?

Some will be excited. They will be thankful for a leader with a clear vision. They will respond well to specific positive and developmental feedback, and will embrace the rewards when you pay off in currency that matters to them.

These people will *move up*. And your organization will be the better for it.

A second group will be afraid. They will fear that the demand for excellence means there will no longer be a place for them on the team. Your job here is to coach, reassure, and be equitable. When this group realizes that standards—and strictures—won't be applied capriciously they, too, will likely be energized.

A third group will be resistant. They will be *incredulous that you are actually asking them to work*, and offended that you think this is reasonable. They will give you excuses and reasons and reasonable excuses. And you'll be tempted to anger, since they aren't buying your vision. Don't give in.

Reset the target. Clearly articulate all of the "whys"—corporate, work group, and personal. Give specific, immediate feedback—both positive and developmental. Pay off in currency that matters to them—both carrot-currency and stick-currency. And watch to see what happens.

When they see that you mean business, a significant percentage of the resisters will get on-board with the new program because you've earned their respect.

Of those remaining, most will leave of their own accord. In essence, you've said, "Get good or get out." And they opt out—which is fine. The balance (those who neither improved nor moved) will have to be "invited to pursue employment opportunities with other companies."

And your team will be the better for all this effort. You demanded excellence—and most of them moved up—either on the first or on subsequent iterations. Those that didn't, moved on—of their own accord or at your impetus. In the end, your team is stronger due to both sets of occurrences.

"Dynamic Tension" Builds More Than Strong Muscles

As a young boy growing up in the late 1950s and early 1960s, I regularly read *Boy's Life* and other magazines for boys my age. And the advertisements were every bit as good as the editorial content.

· One ad particularly fascinated me. It was a torso shot of a well-muscled man without a shirt, and it advertised some fitness program based on "dynamic tension." I never understood dynamic tension in the world of fitness (was it isometric exercises, perhaps?) but I certainly understand it in the world of managerial maxims.

Many of our maxims capture an essential truth, yet can be countered with a directly opposite maxim. This often confuses new managers, whose essential response is: "So—what is it? Black? Or white?" More-seasoned managers look at these young managers with much compassion (and no little amusement) as they answer flatly, "Yes."

There are many truths that can be captured in diametrically opposed maxims. An example: "He who hesitates is lost," can be counterbalanced with, "Fools rush in where angels fear to tread."

"Out of sight, out of mind" contradicts, "Absence makes the heart grow fonder."

"Life is mostly packaging" is offset by, "You can't judge a book by its cover." Which is true? Both. Or neither. It's driven by the circumstances. The paired maxims that we just examined illuminate the law of dynamic tension.

Our Western minds want to drive all thought to one of two poles. Is it black, or is it white? But the truth is often found somewhere in the great middle ground: in the Golden Mean. These paired maxims—"He who hesitates is lost" and "Fools rush in where angels fear to tread"— provide us with anchor points on a decision continuum. We chew over the anchor points, then work our way toward the decision that best fits our current circumstances.

I have a good friend who is passionate, articulate, and perhaps a little crazy. He uses this exact decision-making model when he confronts a problem. "I always like to start at the poles," he says. "I could *do nothing*. Or I could *kill myself*. Then I work in toward the middle."

As you begin to put these maxims into practice in your own managerial and personal life, a couple of cautions are in order.

To a Kid with a New Hammer, Everything Looks Like a Nail

You are going to identify a maxim in this book that you really love. It resonates with who you are and how you were formed. It will become your signature remark. You will *repeat* this maxim all the time, even when it doesn't apply. And that's too bad.

I once worked in the apparel industry. I can tell you that one-size-fits-all is either a lie or a dream. It surely does not fit my lived experience as a shopper or as a manager.

Don't be like a kid with a new hammer. Don't hit every situation with the same maxim. The maxims are not a substitute for your own thinking, your own critical examination of the circumstances you confront. *Instead, the maxims are a starting point for your thinking.* The maxims convey the tribal wisdom from generations of managerial experience. Glean what you can from these offerings, apply it, and leave the rest behind.

If You Keep Doing What You've Been Doing, You'll Keep Getting What You've Been Getting

The saddest place to see this adage illustrated is in the domestic lives of our friends who just can't seem to pick the right marriage partner. Over and over again they bring home partners *exactly* like the one they just got rid of. It leaves us wondering, "How many times are you gonna repeat this experiment?"

We see the same thing in business relationships—both others' and our own. To get different results, we have to do different things. It's as simple (and as *difficult*) as that.

To make more profit, we either have to raise sales volume or cut costs. We can't keep doing what we've been doing. To decrease turnover, we've got to minimize either the things that cause us to dismiss people, or the things that cause them to leave on their own. It's easy to see in the abstract, but difficult to apply.

Why is this so hard? Because it requires *change*. And change is hard. So our challenge—anytime we want to get something different—is three-fold. We must clearly define what we want and how it differs from what we now have. We must examine all our current actions, and see if the actions move us toward this new, revised goal. Ultimately, we must make the changes that will more-nearly assure that we arrive alive at the new and different objective.

Change—in actions, activities, ways of being—is the only option. Because if we keep doing what we've been doing, we'll keep getting what we've been getting.

If You Don't Know What You Stand for, You'll Fall for Anything

Way back in Chapter 6, we established that it is not our job to make value judgments about our employees' motives. And it's not. They weren't raised at our house. It *is* our responsibility in motivating them to pay off in currency that matters to them.

It *is* our job, however, to *fully understand our own motivational profile*, to explore and examine the things that matter most to us, and to make sure they are *ours* (not just some values we picked up by osmosis while swimming around in the American cultural soup).

What *is* it you really stand for? What are your ultimate values? What matters most to you? The lists in Chapter 2 give insight to the key motivators, but most motivators issue from core, ultimate values.

Thus "pursuit of pleasure" is the core value that drives having fun, working less, playing more, and a host of other motivators.

Similarly, "become an accomplished member of the profession" issues forth in learning something new, recognition, looking good to peers, and using new technology.

And the core motivator of "being a faithful member of my religious community" can yield motivators such as making more money (for benevolent giving), doing something that matters, and making a difference.

Many years ago I was responsible for a capital funds campaign for a nonprofit organization that I deeply loved. The organization was a little-known counseling center and fund-raising was difficult. One potential donor offered to make a significant contribution but under shady circumstances. I was tired. It was money. I was tempted to take it.

Then I thought about my core values. This whole deal just didn't feel quite right. I staffed around my weaknesses by seeking counsel from my father, who had a well-developed sense of what's right and what's wrong.

His advice: "I'd run—not walk—away from this deal." I did. And I've never been sorry.

How we live is who we become. Know what you stand for, or you'll fall for anything.

All of our work together has been pointed primarily at management—at asking 'em to work. And now we're gonna look at one final maxim—a maxim that points us to a reality far beyond the workplace.

Your Job Is Not Your Life

Your job may well be your *livelihood*, but it's not your *life*. Your life is the summing-up of your hobbies, your family, your avocations, your outside interests, and your work. Your livelihood is the income-producing work you do to underwrite your life.

It is a common mistake in America: people confuse *what they do* with *who they are*, and this is the genesis of the depression that's endemic to corporate layoffs and downsizing.

Love your work. Take it seriously. Grow as a professional. Become your own best self. But don't get confused: your job is not your life. You are more than your job description. You are more than what you do.

Identify your core values and live out of them for a life that is more than a livelihood.

And while you're at your office, don't forget *The Golden Rules for Managers!*

⟆ MAXIMS ON SHAPING YOUR MANAGEMENT PHILOSOPHY ⟆

A hundred percent of nobody don't like nothing.

No matter what happens, someone will find a way to take it too seriously.

It's okay to ask 'em to work.

Get a commitment.

You can help the people change, or you can change the people.

Don't send your ducks to eagle school.

Once you demand excellence, some people will move up and others will move on—either way, the organization wins.

"Dynamic tension" builds more than strong muscles.

To a kid with a new hammer, everything looks like a nail.

If you keep doing what you've been doing, you'll keep getting what you've been getting.

If you don't know what you stand for, you'll fall for anything.

Your job is not your life.

QUESTIONS FOR REFLECTION

1. How do you handle it when employees dislike your decisions? How about when your management dislikes your decisions? What can you do to put yourself at ease with the notion that a hundred percent of nobody don't like nothing?

2. Are you good at getting a commitment? Why did you answer as you did? How could you improve?

3. "You can help the people change, or you can change the people." What is your response to this maxim? Have you ever "cared more than they care?" What was the outcome?

4. How can you demand excellence in a way that your employees will want to *move up* and not *move on*? What can you do to minimize fear? How can you make sure the target is clear? How will you pay off in currency that matters to them?

CHALLENGE FOR APPLICATION

How can you more directly ask your people to work without being brutal, but without being wishy-washy either? What upsides do you see? Are there any potential downsides?

ENDNOTES

Chapter 1: Vision and Planning

1. David P. Campbell, *If You Don't Know Where You're Going, You'll Probably End Up Somewhere Else* (Allen, TX: Argus Communications, 1974).

Chapter 2: Motivation

1. Hayes and Associates, *Managing Employee Performance* (Winston-Salem, NC: Hayes and Associates, 1985), Unit 4.

2. J. Frank McNair, *Leadership and Management SuccesSkills* (Winston-Salem, NC: McNair & McNair, 1999), 17.

3. Ibid., 18.

Chapter 4: Coaching

1. Robert W. Pike, *Creative Training Techniques Handbook* (Minneapolis: Lakewood Books, 1989), 3.

2. Emmie H. Alexander and Jerry T. Hancock, *Performance*

Management (Davidson, NC: Alexander/Hancock Associates, 1995).

Chapter 5: Feedback and Performance Management

1. J. Frank McNair, *Supervisory SuccesSkills* (Winston-Salem, NC: McNair & McNair, 1995), 7–4.

Chapter 7: Relationship Management

1. James E. Kroncke and J. Frank McNair, *The LEAD Program Workbook* (Winston-Salem, NC: Kroncke Consulting/LTM Associates, 1991), 26.

INDEX

ABOUT THE AUTHOR

Frank McNair started learning *The Golden Rules for Managers* as a child—asking questions of both his father and his granddaddy as they talked about managing the family businesses they ran.

Frank began his corporate life with First Citizens Bank and Trust, then worked in sales and marketing for RJ Reynolds Industries and the L'eggs Division of Sara Lee Corporation. In his last position in the corporate world, Frank was director of sales and marketing (all product lines) for Douglas Battery Company.

Since 1988, Frank and his wife, Laura, have been partners in McNair & McNair—a full-service training and consulting business that specializes in helping companies get the best possible results from their employee team. Their clients include Amarr Garage Doors, The Connor Group, Ferrari North America, General Dynamics, Krispy Kreme Doughnut Corporation, Volvo Trucks, Planters-LifeSavers, and Wake Forest University. You can find out more about McNair & McNair at www.mcnairandmcnair.com.

A graduate of the University of North Carolina, Frank was a Morehead Scholar. He holds an MBA from the Babcock Graduate School of Management at Wake Forest University.

In addition to *The Golden Rules for Managers*, Frank has written *How You Make the Sale*, which was published by Sourcebooks in October 2005. You can find out more about *How You Make the Sale* and order a copy at www.howyoumakethesale.com.

Frank is active in his community of faith. He studied at the Oratory in Rock Hill, South Carolina, and completed their Horizons of the Spirit program in 1993. He has done graduate work at the General Theological Seminary of the Episcopal Church in New York City, and in 2002 he completed the Certificate in Spiritual Formation at Columbia (Presbyterian) Theological Seminary in Atlanta, Georgia.

In his non-work life, Frank enjoys sailing, waterskiing, working out, and reading. He is a graduate of the North Carolina Outward Bound School and was an Eagle Scout. He is married to Laura McNair, the love of his life and his business partner. They share a home overlooking the woods with Gracie, a golden retriever and Molly Brown, a chocolate lab.

Frank McNair delights in helping groups, individuals, and organizations solve their problems and move forward to successfully achieve their goals. Frank can serve as a sounding board, a coach, and a mentor, or he can partner with your organization on a comprehensive training initiative or an ongoing consulting project. You can contact Frank directly through his website at www.frankmcnair.com.

THE ULTIMATE SALES-SUCCESS GUIDE FROM FRANK MCNAIR!

Kirkus Reviews called it "Invaluable"—and YOU WILL TOO!

ISBN 978-1-4022-0435-7

If you are a salesperson, manage salespeople, or have salespeople in your company, *How You Make the Sale* is the book for you! Frank McNair demystifies selling and points you to key steps that will make the sales process less painful and more successful for everyone involved.

This book is perfect as a text for sales training and is invaluable for managers who need to understand how sales works so they can effectively manage a sales team. It is also a great refresher read for long-term salespeople who need to get back to the basics that made them successful in the first place.

Available wherever books are sold
Bulk Order Call Direct (630) 961-3900